DO I STILL NEED MY HEAD EXAMINED OR JUST A NEW PAIR OF RUNNING SHOES?

Mitchell Milch LCSW

ISBN: 0692818405
ISBN 13: 9780692818404

DEDICATION

*I dedicate this memoir to those who helped me find and re-find my "self"
and my way, time and time again. How fortunate I have been for your
growth stimuli. You provided the impetuses for me to self-organize, and to
integrate my heart, soul and mind, so I might strive to be an ambassador
of health and well-being. I am eternally grateful to all you steadfast
guardians of faith in my being, this ineffable artistic work-in-progress.
I could have never stayed the course of rewriting my personal narrative
without you.*

*The soundtrack for this improvised reality series continues at intervals
to be an unintelligible cacophony of discordant sounds and jumble of
indiscernible tempos and rhythms on the edge of completely falling apart.
Who can explain how paradoxically this never-complete concerto of sorts
has for some time now been "good enough" and over time "getting better"?*

*To my delight, every rewrite cuts a wider swathe of inspiration and
empowerment. How can this one time "sissy boy" repay you for becoming
a man who now "never says die" to the unending challenge of making
meaning of the moment?*

*For those of you who cherish your privacy I will not blow your covers as
the secret agents who guarded my quest to debunk the fiction that my
fingerprints on this universe did not matter. With this memoir, I pay
tribute to all of you, my wise and humble angels. Thank you! Your names
are inscribed in my soul for eternity in homage to your generous hearts.*

All my love to Dr. G., Dr. L., Dr. T., Dr. B., Dr. Bob, Mana L., Dr. Gary T., and cousin and friend Bob B. Special thanks goes to my developmental editor, Garth Sundem, for reorganizing and focusing this once itinerant ensemble of tangent-happy story lines. Finally, I wish to recognize my boundlessly generous and skillful publishing professional of a wife for her expert assistance in editing this memoir.

FORWARD

This brave story, written with pathos, humor and rich detail, will delight readers, regardless of whether they are psychoanalysts like Milch. It is a moving, insightful account of one man's journey to overcome his traumatic childhood and the shame, self-doubt and fraught sense of masculinity it left behind. Thanks to the author's commendable openness, "Do I Still Need My Head Examined or Just a New Pair of Running Shoes?" is a testament to resilience and the strength of the human spirit."

– Eric Sherman, author of "Notes from the Margins: The Analysts Subjectivity in the Treatment Setting."

In his memoir, social worker-psychoanalyst, Mitchell Milch, places himself and the significant others in his life under a high-resolution microscope to elucidate psychoanalytic truisms and assist his readers in freeing themselves from "toxic unconscious habits" that are endlessly and destructively repeated. Using himself as the model of a man chained by the forces of his past, he seeks to demonstrate how he succeeded in breaking a previously uninterrupted chain of intergenerational trauma while living life and going through a series of psychoanalytic treatments. These treatments led him to understand that we cling "to patently false and unprocessed assumptions as if they were guideposts for effective living arrived at through extensive empirical research." This book is not in any way a dry psychoanalytic text, but rather a living, breathing memoir whose "characters" come off the page as genuine, true-to-life flawed, but real human beings. Milch's writing is unsparingly frank, filled with a sardonic humor and an ability to look at himself with an almost brutal honesty. As with a psychoanalytic treatment, as you read this memoir you will laugh and cry and learn a lot in the process.

– Linda B. Sherby, Ph.D., ABPP, is a psychologist-psychoanalyst in practice in Boca Raton, Florida. She is the author of the book, Love and Loss in Life and in Treatment, published by Routledge in 2013. This book combines memoir with Dr. Sherby's work with patients, demonstrating how the analyst's present life circumstances affects her patients and the treatment. She co-authored the book Getting Free: Women and Psychotherapy, and has written numerous published papers including "Love and Hate in the Treatment of Borderline Patients" and "Countertransference Love." She also writes a blog, "Inside/Outside," which addresses the complex relationship between patient and therapist.

INTRODUCTION

I lived much of my life fearful that I would not transcend my developmental traumas and my life would end without honor and distinction. Had I truly believed that my life was a gift and that my parents' sacrifices for me was not a backbreaking burden of filial duty to make them proud, I might not have lived my early life as I had, on the edge of panic that my legacy would not qualify as a footnote in any history book. The concept that I had washed my hands for eternity of their lifetime unhappiness in some wash basin installed in my hovel in Hell was a fate over which my gastrointestinal tract shed tears of inflammation daily.

It is rather sad when a 10-year-old's defense against unrelenting environmental stress is to create a quasi-delusion that he has undiagnosed and thus untreated stomach cancer. In all humility, this was a brilliant solution for ending my misery and perhaps avoiding a sentence to rot in Hell for the moral crime of failure to fix my parents' miserable lives with some dazzling good works. In this age of delivery-on-demand, I might have jumped at the opportunity to return my gift of life and taken advantage of a user-friendly return policy.

In this memoir you will read about my intemperate parents whose emotions blew through my life like gale force winds and merited recognition with names like Tropical Storm Ruth or

Hurricane Abe. Their intemperate inputs added to my already anxious temperament. Emotions are contagious and theirs for me were like intravenous amphetamines on top of multiple cups of coffee. Reality felt like living on the edge of annihilation. My end might come as a tidal wave of emotional stress to swallow me up without leaving a trace of me in its wake. A compatible alternative might be that I go the way of an automobile engine stressed to the point that its metal components degrade into an inert pile of molten junk.

In other words, my home life was not exactly the vacation destination one might choose to decompress. In fact, when I am asked the obvious question—"When did you start running?"—the surprising answer was some point in time that predated my entrance into Kindergarten. I started running for my life as a bulwark against losing my mind. Necessity was the mother of this ingenious invention that ensured my survival early on and later guaranteed I would not do much better than survive for decades. This prepubescent's adaptive efforts to master developmental traumas later became this postpubescent's maladaptive strategy to relinquish control of my life to primitive and involuntary survival mechanisms of the brain that tripped false alarms with nary an immediate cause for concern.

This memoir is my search to answer the following question: How can we understand that I broke a previously uninterrupted chain of causation that was a domino-like, transmission of traumas large and small from one generation to another? My fervent wish is that you benefit from witnessing my process of rewriting my personal narrative. You may reasonably ask yourself what took this guy so long to get his act together? The honest response is "I'm not sure but I do come by my slowness of foot honestly." Perhaps you will shed some light on this matter for yourself.

The buck would not have stopped with me had I not zealously and passionately investigated and rewritten themes that previously bound my narrative to my ancestors' static ones. I pass this memoir forward to you as an expression of loving gratitude for the quality of my treatment providers "being" with me over the course of three plus decades. Together we unpacked and deconstructed my relationships to family, running, and my not so adult, adult romantic pursuits. My shrinks helped set the context to orchestrate a process, and develop the infrastructure for a laboratory to reimagine and reinvent myself. Over time, I was able on my own to replicate the conditions for such a laboratory. I have turned this glorified diary into a vehicle to enhance and advance my work as a patient, analyst, husband, father, athlete, writer, and friend.

The purpose of inviting you to accompany me on these journeys is to seed your imagination with the potential possibilities for what is entirely and understandably counter-intuitive: to find and embrace a way to love, nurture and make amenable to benevolent control the so-called inner enemies of your peace and happiness. These are preconditions for harnessing the plasticity of your brain. My brain's learned mobility and flexibility are the performance metrics that have freed me up to proactively express my creative voice in joyful and meaningful adaptation to changing circumstances. These same metrics determined my success moving through space with greater efficiency and ease of movement. Another way to put this is to point out the direct correspondence between rewiring my brain and the conversion of dammed-up, diverted and wasted potential creative energy into actual useful energy.

My relentless drive to justify my right "to be me," free of concern about who might want me to do for them what only adults can do for themselves—to rescue and repair their damaged nervous systems—has been a constant throughout my life.

This work of personal transformation has been an ultramarathon. It is one I never could have imagined I could develop the endurance, patience, and resilience to injury to pursue. One does not sprint before one learns to jog, and one does not truly learn to jog until one can walk without a disability that prevents locomotion. I had to complete a process of rehabilitation before I could develop my athletic potential and overcome my chronic creative constipation.

No one will ever mistakenly confuse me with an outlier. That is my ace of spades as a force of empowerment and inspiration. I spent 11 years writing this memoir on top of 23 years of psychoanalytic treatment prior to this project's inception in search of what I was born with and subsequently lost sight of; my connection to the ineffable and infinite forces of creation. At age 27, I had lost my way. At age 62, I have accomplished everything I set out to accomplish on my bucket list, and the sky continues to be the limit as long as I keep on trucking. Did I need my head examined, just a new pair of running shoes—or maybe something else? Let's find out!

TABLE OF CONTENTS

CHAPTER 1

DO I STILL NEED MY HEAD EXAMINED OR JUST A NEW PAIR OF RUNNING SHOES?

This is my story. It is a story of discovery and change. It is also a story about running. I began running regularly in 1973 at the age of 19 and have continued to run regularly for the past 43 years. We are talking about hundreds and hundreds of pairs of running shoes. The result is that I can take to the roads on any given day and for a few precious moments compress time to nothing, so that my full sensory experience of running at 62 is virtually indistinguishable from the memories of running in Brooklyn, New York on those summers home from college. It is as if the memories come rushing back with the speed of love.

But this priceless gift of my relationship to running is only the tip of the iceberg of reasons for writing this book. Yes, running is a keepsake with extraordinary sentimental value—an enduring focal point that sums up in one compelling image my reasons for being—the thread that held me together, held me back, moved me forward and was a cocoon I jettisoned when this spiritual butterfly was ready to fly on his own. But this book also chronicles dramatic personality changes through the process of psychoanalysis and self-discovery.

I had been searching for, nurturing, reinventing, and expressing a vision for a loving, fulfilled and happy self since I had entered psychotherapy in 1981. This vision grew from the seeds of a sense of well-being derived from the experience of running, and my efforts to replicate this experience without having to first run 8-10 miles. During my asphalt-pounding days this sense of well-being was short lived. Even though training helped me hone so many much-needed traits to succeed in other spheres of my life, these skills (much to my head-banging chagrin for decades) did not translate well in the arenas of love and work. My poorly understood fears of success and failure kept me torn between running for decades, both away from my self and toward self-awareness. I eventually moved forward sometimes sideways and sometimes on my knees, but I moved forward nonetheless.

Still, if you are an avid runner who wants to believe that a discussion of your training diary is more interesting than listening to a faucet drip, this book is not for you. That's right, you runners out there will be starved of golden nuggets on how to stay in the race and not lose valuable minutes when Mother Nature calls. After wrestling with myself I have even begged off including a chapter on how to keep your non-running loved ones awake while you share recent entries from your running diary. In this book, you will not find one reference to the sexiest outfits a runner might wear to pick up a fellow runner in the hopes of cross training in bed. You will not find one tidbit about exotic race settings or even the latest breakthroughs on how to prevent chafing of your inner thighs while marathon training during the dog days of summer. Finally, I will not offer any proprietary formulas to calculate how many miles one needs to run each week to work off pints of Haagen Dazs chocolate ice cream. I cross my heart and hope to be stuck raising freshly minted adolescents the rest of my life if I am not true to this pledge.

If, however, you are a runner who has stopped long enough in front of his mirror at 5:00 AM to question why you are out running for the 20th consecutive day when your lover is squirming with desire in bed, your body is crying out for rest, your spouse needs help to get the kids ready for school, or you have an unfinished presentation at work to give in a few short hours, then this book may be exactly what the shrink ordered. I have had my head examined on some pretty ratty couches in my time, so a case could be made that I needed to find a competent shrink to dissuade me from wasting my time and yours writing a book about running that scrupulously avoids anything to do with training, racing or injury prevention and management. How about that for a marketing strategy!

In other words, the success of this book will be measured by the number of readers who can count on their fingers the number of times they broke a sweat running for anything except perhaps a train, a beer in their refrigerator during a commercial break, or when their children impulsively ran into the street and put themselves in harm's way.

The good news is that I am sufficiently removed from my days of overly identifying with my fitness level and modest running speed to laugh at myself for having been so narrow minded in my obsession with this activity. I was very much a one-trick pony for many years. Running was as much my tragic flaw as it was my road to salvation. I am a recovering running junkie who will make many shameful and embarrassing admissions about my own irrational behaviors during the course of the following chapters.

If you are anything like me, meaning a Homo sapiens, then you too have, or at least know someone who has, spent enough emotional energies fighting, denying, evading, minimizing, and turning a blind eye to the truths of your life to illuminate a major U.S. city for many a moonless night. It has been my life's mission to end this war with myself. It has been staged inside and outside psychoanalysts' offices as many times as, let's say, *A Streetcar Named Desire* has been staged in amateur and professional theaters in this country since its debut on Broadway in 1951. I have toted around emotional baggage equivalent to that of a middle-class European family of four's luggage. Having worked at the Grand Hyatt New York as a bellman in an earlier incarnation, I know that is a lot of baggage to inventory and secure in an orderly fashion so that the contents do not embarrassingly, shamefully and guiltily spill out of their containers and create problems for others who might be innocent victims. Unfair or otherwise, no matter how much more competent I have become at the mechanics and logistics of baggage packing, unpacking and transit, the management of my emotional baggage is a lifelong proposition that keeps me paying for my shrink's real estate investments.

I am someone very late to be invited to "adults only" parties, and even later to be invited to any VIP parties in the cordoned-off areas where mindful adults hang out. If I thought it would help my first wife mourn the failure of our marriage, I might say to her today: "You were quite prescient in your hopes of me becoming the man you wished me to be, except we both miscalculated the length of the trip by about the time it takes to drive a few hundred thousand miles on a gearless bicycle." Somehow I do not think it would help her at this stage to consider that rehabilitating my fearful emotional paralysis was a process that took longer than our most depressing estimates.

Other than my relationships with my brother Peter, sister-in-law Lois, and first cousin Bob (some names have been changed to protect privacy), running has been my most enduring, and in bygone times, my closest relationship. Do you need any more evidence than this embarrassing and shameful admission that I needed my head examined? If I had ever owned a pet, which I have not, this book might have been about my dog or cat. Until my daughter Jocelyn brought home a hamster named Sandy when she was seven, the only other living things my family cohabitated with were cockroaches...and they were not bought at an animal shelter or pet store. On the contrary they could have been disciples of the greatest marauders the world has ever known, Genghis Khan and Attila the Hun, who would have been proud of them. They invaded our apartment in 1963 and evicted us in short order. They were hard enough to track, let alone leash, so they did not quite qualify as pets.

If I had developed a yen for drugs or alcohol in the late 1960s, or had continued to collect stamps beyond the age of eight, this book might have been about those relationships. It might have been about my first love, my brother, my best friend growing up, or even a shoe fetish, had I ever developed one. It could have certainly been about my relationship to eating and my on-again, off-again love affair with being skinny. Instead, this book is largely about my family.

I do not sound anything like my father anymore who somehow mistook his mouth as an anus and suffered from incessant bouts of verbal diarrhea that left us with a stench of shame. Yet the older I get, the more my facial features resemble his. And I persist in having recurring "shame" dreams, where I am back in college unprepared to take my final exams or lost on my way to the exam rooms. After decades of psychoanalysis I am still beset by anal spasms which are residual neurotic symptoms of my mother anxiously forcing a toilet training regimen on me, and I am still capable of re-living abandonment fears when patients abruptly leave my practice without explanation, causing me to throw into question my competence as a therapist.

In truth, if this book earns attention it will be largely due to it being a raw, unvarnished confessional that may have some loved ones cursing under their breath and wishing I used a pen name while leaving their homes under cover of darkness, sufficiently embarrassed by this" tell all." Honestly, those who might feel violated will in all likelihood not dignify its publication and if they do, may be surprised or even saddened that assigning a pseudonym to them robbed them of their deserved acknowledgment. In many cases I have deleted all geographical references to my story so as not to offer any would-be hound dogs a scent to sniff at.

I am supremely confident that this book will do a lot more good than harm, so I will let the chips fall where they may.

As well, you probably think this shrink will bore you to death with theory and intellectual abstractions. Granted, you may hear a few buzzwords like brain plasticity, mindfulness, emotional attunement, compromise formation, and the compulsion to repeat history. Please bear with me as I will use them sparingly and only in the service of making one over-arching point: If we learn to mindfully construct our understanding of ourselves and the universe moment by moment, context by context, and remain open to reinterpreting and correcting the artificially self-limiting lessons of history, we can become art forms of our own making, pregnant with possibilities for meaningful self-expression. We cannot be reborn and start over in terms of beginning the life cycle anew and undo traumas that may predate by generations our emergence from the birth canal. However, it is my proposition that getting one's head examined may be like learning to re-parent ourselves: we might learn to harness our imaginations as playgrounds, where we give birth to new forms and functions for the remainder of our conscious years. Could it get any better than that?

In the early 1990s, when I started my psychoanalytic training, I could not imagine having a thriving private practice or graduating as a psychoanalyst. Equally, I could not have imagined enjoying a successful marriage. And yet today, I am the first member of my family to be a published author. Sometimes I look in the mirror and wonder who let this complete stranger into our home.

I could not have written this book any earlier in my life. There are some admissions herein that might have been too painful for me to connect to and reflect on earlier.

How I have related to running is how I have related to my life. Running has been my sorcerer, my mentor, my mistress, my parent, my best friend, my worst enemy, my most cherished hobby, my purgatory, my addiction, and anything else I have left out that one could conjure up. This relationship has changed me over time, and I have in turn changed it. I have laced on new pairs of running shoes and have braved wind, rain, sleet, hail, snow, frigid temperature, and hellaciously warm temperatures for over four decades. I never gave up on running just as I never gave up on life, and this is no accident.

I might have given up on both if not for the folks whose psychoanalytic couches I have sat and laid on for 30 plus years. These folks have been full of wisdom, inspiration, kindness, compassion, and humility in equal parts. They simply refused to let me give up on myself. For gifting me a future worth working towards, I dedicate this book to them. I thank D.G., Ph.D., E.K., Ph.D., M.L., Ph.D., and C.T., Ph.D., for convincing me that I needed my head examined over and over again to revise and re-transcribe the lessons of history that left me with a very limited, rigid, and ineffective repertoire of coping strategies.

As you read the following chapters, I hope you will be curious enough to begin reflecting on the potential learning value of the information and energies tied up in the bonds of your most enduring and cherished relationships. I tell you this to stretch your minds in thinking about the relationships in your lives that might open doors you may have closed prematurely or resisted reopening. My wish is that this memoir inspires you to launch a new search for answers on how to free yourselves from toxic unconscious habits that have run your lives in rigidly repetitive ways, like a needle stuck on an old phonograph playing the same melodic interval over and over again.

CHAPTER 2

NOT QUITE POETRY IN MOTION

On June 9th, 1973 during an interval of just over two minutes, Ron Turcotte and his horse Secretariat made time slow down. The 100,000-plus in attendance at Belmont Park raised the amplitude of the wave of momentum horse and rider rode. The pair looked as if they flipped a switch and kicked into gear a plan so grand and yet so effortlessly organic in its precision. On command, their highly rehearsed instructions sets were retrieved from memory and executed flawlessly. The eyes of the sports world were on the yin and yang of environmental forces at one moment or another in opposition to the synchronized efforts of horse and rider to master them. The breathtaking outcome unfolded as a compromise of accommodation and adaptation to these forces at work. This dynamic duo remind me of the once-relevant Tiger Woods smashing stinger shots that cut through cross currents of wind as if their trajectories were undisturbed, like a bullet shot out of a high power rifle.

The tandem moved past their rival Sham as if he stood still, a stationery prop that moved in and out of awareness like scenery flashes in and then immediately out of a field of vision as a passenger on an Acela Amtrak train. The duo was so dialed into their well-rehearsed chess moves that they looked as unperturbed by the crowd as if all alone on a Utah salt flat. The horse was a masterpiece of grace, power, speed, determination and fearlessness in spite of the size of the stage and historicity of the moment.

I remember fondly Chick Hearn's call of the run that capped Secretariat's historic Triple Crown victory in 1973. It was a wearisome kind of summer day, when moving through humid air was like slogging through a swamp with heavy boots. Right before the three-quarter mile pole, Secretariat opened up a 12-lengths lead over his fierce rival Sham, a lead he would widen to 25 lengths by the finish line. Hearn remarked: "He is moving like a tremendous machine." I can still recall the goose bumps that erupted on my arms as I watched this race for the ages. This was nothing short of a full-body spiritual orgasm. I could not at the time define and articulate what the vibrations coursing through me meant. Secretariat ran as if he defied the atmospheric conditions under which everyone else labored. The horse and rider crossed the 1.5-mile finish line looking as if they had a lot more left in the tank. Together, Ron Turcotte and the horse they called "Big Red" set a world record for 1.5 miles by over two seconds. Their world record Belmont Stakes time still stands, 43 years later.

At that stage of my life, I could not put into words my body's veneration of what I longed to emulate. This horse was without equal in innate cardiovascular gifts, response to training, and responsiveness to his rider's improvisational genius. This three-year-old squeezed every last succulent drop of performance from his potential yield of nectar, something that generations of Type A personalities like myself will chase in vain and never achieve. Simply put, this animal was the personification of what it meant to maximize the utility of the lived moment. How ironic that without awareness of doing so, I projected onto this horse my prescient future ego ideal: unselfconscious trust in a collaboratively engineered, mindful self, and faith in service to ineffable processes and forces operating outside my awareness. I could not imagine at age 19 ½ so foreign a quality of being, and yet it beckoned me and my full attention like some sorceress. Secretariat made it look easy and I took the bait.

This captivating, legendary horse guaranteed that the purchase of my first pair of running shoes would not be my last.

Why did this great horse so inspire me to run? Let me count the ways. Much of my inspiration to run like Secretariat was a defensive reaction to the depressive pall that hung over my family home. My parents established a hostile pattern of engagement that might best be described as a chaotic and destructive dyadic personality, so rigid in its unpredictable predictability.

The best metaphor I can muster for such predictable chaos is as follows: In an abandoned home the furniture left intact has three inches of dust resting on the upholstery. There is no air circulating in this mausoleum-like monument to the past. Suddenly a window is opened on a windy day and a gust of energy is introduced. The entropy in the room is astounding as chaos ensues and dust flies everywhere in hard-to-fathom directions. Suddenly, the window is closed, and within several hours the room appears as if no outside energy has ever been introduced.

Our family subsisted on a steady diet of endless cycles of victimization and revenge. Please pardon my endless litany of food metaphors. I came by my oral fixation honestly. These were mirthless and hopelessly depressing scenes that left me feeling ashamed and undeserving of happiness for not stopping the carnage. I lived in silent penance for my sinister wish that Dad leave, yet clear as a bell about the truth that egress could only be achieved over the other's dead body. Each possessed the immutable belief that he or she could not live without the other.

As much as things changed in my home, in the end nothing shifted one iota. My parents continued to pursue the impossible, to break free of each other's orbits while attempting to control the source of the gravitational pulls over them. I had no way of understanding the logic that dictated the timing and unfolding of these dance moves, which left me desperately hurt and depressed. I was inspired by Secretariat to run, hoping to generate enough speed and power to overcome the gravitational pull of my parent's depressive atmospheric orbit. How I might fare in this gravity-less environment on the heels of my developmental achievement was the million-dollar question.

I wanted desperately to be in bullet-like velocity, the antithesis of their sluggish, depressive natures. If you can imagine the protesting groan of a locomotive's rusted steel powered up to move after extended idleness, then you can imagine what moving through space was like for my parents. If people of faith believe that their bodies are the temples of their souls, then my parents were atheists. They treated their bodies as if their souls were those picked-over garments you see on closeout tables in department store basements. As they got older, moving became more and more difficult. Secretariat was everything they were not. Anytime anyone called attention to my parents' deficiencies, my parents affixed an invisible bull's eye on the chest of the perceived agitant and dressed this person down for deigning to insinuate that they lacked anything in comparison to anyone. If they ever conceded to be un-Secretariat-like, responsibility for this state of affairs sat squarely in the laps of those whose feeble provisions were likewise no fault of their own. How did anyone dare be so depraved as to think of them as responsible for anything that was less than perfect? How could anyone justly hold them accountable for their fat-laden bodies bred early in life or for them taking an eye for an eyelash if the plucked eyelash felt like an eye-gouging?

To remain in this toxic environment was the emotional equivalent of being damaged beyond repair by exposure to acid rain. This was a family system frozen in time and space. The footprints of the past were part and parcel of the amplitude of their dramatic physical and emotional gyrations. With my crisis-oriented neural grooves reinforced to the point of being ravine-like, I ran the risk of walking through the world like a war veteran fearful of stepping on landmines. I was damned if I reflected poorly on my parents, and damned if they felt I showed them up. If I ever achieved Secretariat's dynamic ease and freedom of movement, and made the powerful thrusts of my legs look easy, I had best do so somewhere out of my parents' sight.

In some ways, I paradoxically saw in Secretariat a path to my parents' redemption. Their hilariously wishful logic was that their pronounced dearth of character strengths would not prevent them from imparting to me "the right stuff." This fairy tale of their imaginations had me then shower them with pride and joy, and redeem all the sacrifices they felt compelled to make as dictated by their own "blameless" parents.

I did not appear early on to have "the right stuff" to make my astronaut dreams realities. I lacked the intrepid aggressiveness of callow male youths, which left me more like a female object of male domination than a powerful male conquistador. The most searing symbol of this was on full display when I played baseball. My body would go limp from an over infusion of stress hormones when it was my turn to bat. I went as limp as a guy who suffered with erectile dysfunction problems in bed. Performance anxiety is the great destroyer of coordination, rhythm and balance. Just ask any professional golfer in contention for a major championship on the back nine of the final round how easily they are betrayed by jacked up nervous systems.

During childhood I dreamed about shadowy forms in pursuit of my naked form. I would try to run away but my legs wobbled uncontrollably as if semi-paralyzed by fear. My interpretation of these dreams is that I return to earlier times in my life to master fears that my naked aggression towards my brother and father over their failure to admire the creative fruits of my agency put me in mortal danger.

My father, in denial of his vengeful motivations, somehow found it cute to mortify me by drawing attention to my small penis after setting me up by allowing me as a young child to run around naked. I think comparing our phallic appendages buoyed his fragile ego by subjecting me to the cruel interactions he too suffered as a child and had not forgiven, so as to return the favor a generation later. Such humiliations left me literally sapped of any strength in my body as I got caught between my impotent desires to one day triumph over my father and dance on his grave in victory, and my fears that I could mortally wound him or if he survived, turn him into a wounded animal out to destroy me and condemn me as a depraved child.

In other words, I was the antithesis of the image of Secretariat stretched out in full flight like a large phallus primed for an orgasm. I still joke about how I would stand in the dry and traction-less batter's box of my Little League Days without cleats thinking that the weight of my batter's helmet might topple me over. If I were fortunate enough to hit the ball on the ground, I made the infielders look like Gold Glovers in the box scores. No matter how badly handcuffed they might be by my slowly hit balls, it took me so long to run the 90 feet to first base that even if they booted the ball several times and threw the ball on a parabolic trajectory, I was still out by a mile.

I secretly wished to be the daughter my father always wanted me to be. In generations past there were fewer opportunities and expectations for girls to express their athleticism. Necessity being the mother of my own wishful thinking as modeled by my parents, I clutched a fatal assumption that I would not be loved and respected in my own right unless I became some iconic-like figure with a golden aura they could bask in and take credit for. Hey, if my own parents demanded this of me what would have made me think the universe would expect less? Women of my mother's generation were not expected to compete for seats in the corporate board-room. Had I been born female, might I have been spared mano-a-mano testosterone infused financial wars, waged to the death.

I tried to live up to the image my father wanted me to inhabit so he could live vicariously through me and feel entitled to take credit for my successes, even though he was of little help on the journey. This was a means to feel close to him. It was also a way for me to stave off ridicule for any tastes, preferences, or yearnings that would thwart his designs on me.

Projective identification is a fancy term for finding a way to escape being locked in a phone booth with a part of you bent on belittling yourself. You can expel it from the phone booth but until you learn to be present and develop a benevolent observing self, you remain tethered to it and at its mercy, powerless but to react in conditioned ways, no matter how many times you project these part objects onto others. Such mindless emotion is blind, and it is nuance and subtlety free. When primordial, hard-wired survival instincts kick in as they do when emotions bias overly negative perceptions, the commission of a sin colors the sinner as the enemy. Like an old golf teaching professional of mine, Bob Marlin, used to say half kiddingly, "If I get mad, someone's going to the hospital." Fortunately for me, I took that threat to heart and tiptoed around him. If I was not sleeping with the enemy next to me in bed, then only one rather porous and flimsily constructed plaster board wall separated my bedroom from the bedroom occupied by my parents, potential enemies created by my inflamed emotions. It behooved me to run and situate myself at a safe distance from this home at the earliest possibility, as a raging inferno of devastation could be ignited by as little as one carelessly lit word or deed.

There was as much reality in my universe to anyone clawing, and crawling, one's way toward success as there was once life beyond the lens of the most powerful telescope. So, when my road to success did not follow the footsteps of Fred Astaire, who danced through a sound set replica of a Pittsburgh coal mine and emerged unstained by soot and sweat, I felt like an abject failure. There was no poetic flow of a personal narrative coming to life as I moved through space and time. I had not been hatched yet as an observing and reflecting presence capable of reinterpreting my story.

Dad believed that gifted athletes, scholars, and the like, were born or groomed early on for success. Winners were like Robert Redford's character in the film "The Natural." They might take their talents out of mothballs any time and express their gifts without skipping a beat. Losers struggled to master skills, sweated their frustrations and confusions, had their spirits broken by humiliation for needing help, and ultimately put themselves out of their misery and gave up. My father never integrated the struggle for mastery into a valued self-image. It did not exist in his consciousness, and his gospel became my gospel as well.

Early on, running was an exercise in futility that took the mindful pen, which would allow me to later rewrite my narrative, right out of my hand. So much energy and information formerly trapped in my soma was with regularity freed and discharged to the gates of my consciousness while running that it received no more than a passing thought before dispersing into the atmosphere beyond future recognition. Here on a silver platter was the essence of the old scripts that outside my awareness took on lives of their own, broke down the door to my executive cockpit, and assumed control of me. Had I already embarked on my walk towards enlightenment, I would like to believe that I would have taken myself more seriously. I would have made mental notes to reflect on after my run. Then, I would have rewritten these narratives that required reinterpretation to free up the assertion of my right to reclaim my pilot's seat.

As such, Secretariat represented the allure of achieving my "mythical" potential and so earning the right to be loved by my parents and happy with myself. Absent any desire for transgender surgery, running was my microsurgery free way of reattaching the penis to my castrated male identity. It was decades before I removed my blinders while lying on Dr. K's couch and realized that this idea that I was destined for greatness at anything was pure fiction.

Running was a stroke of unconscious genius in my efforts to resolve my conflict over growing up. At first, my running form was a rather uncoordinated and muscle-challenged series of movements. I was a Pillsbury Dough Boy impersonator waddling around SUNY Binghamton's indoor track. No one who watched my jiggling fat cells confused me with a personified version of the Statue of David. Poetry in motion I was not. This was not performance art worth exhibiting in public unless I was looking for a belly laugh at my own expense.

Soon running became a behaviorally conditioned response that took on a mindless life of its own. Eventually it became an addiction – a complex set of symptoms that told a story of literally and figuratively running away from internal and external images of my parents who saw me as an accident waiting to happen absent their belittling directives.

There was as much reality to how I saw myself and what I hoped to accomplish as there is reality to the cocaine addict looking to recapitulate the pain-free high of first using cocaine long after this pursuit has cost him his job, his home, and his family. I quote Lennon and McCarthy to aptly describe myself as having been a "Nowhere Man." I was nowhere and did not know I was not anchored for more than a fleeting moment in the present. Most often I wanted to jump out of my skin, as being present and alone with myself was much too distressing. Running was a means to discharge through movement energies that endlessly triggered emotional flashbacks to traumatic events. My mind, my gastrointestinal tract, and my immune system were stuck in heightened states of crisis alert. This was a chronically unhealthy state of affairs. Trauma is like a self-generating, self-replicating cancer. Until I learned to re-regulate my nervous system and neutralize these false-positive internal alarms, I went nowhere very fast in my efforts to discharge excess neural excitation. When the floodwaters of anxiety provoking emotions forever swell, then running is like using a bucket to bail water out of a row boat rife with holes—a losing proposition.

I insulated myself from the crazy-making confusion and self-doubt that arose from experiences that flew in the face of what I had been taught earlier in life. I did what my coaches told me to do and if my body told me otherwise, I did not listen. In my falsely dichotomous world, you either knew what you were doing or you did not. If you did not, you were screwed. More was better than less, and even more than that was better. An autonomous self, I learned, could not be trusted. I did not dare question the fallacies that I had been pressured by parents to hold as self-evident. Otherwise, normal states of confusion might throw one of us, and then perhaps, all of us into states of anxious chaos. So I kept my skepticism over what I had been taught vacuum-sealed and rigged with high-security psychological defenses.

These lies fortified an identity that had as much integrity as a house of cards.

CHAPTER 3

TOO MUCH OF ANYTHING CAN BE WORSE THAN THE PROBLEM IT IS TRYING TO SOLVE

In September 1972, my parents dropped me off with a magician-worthy-sized trunk at SUNY Binghamton. It was my first overnight separation from my parents, and the first time in my life I had no one to answer to except myself for more than a few hours. My parents' expectation that I could suddenly be responsible for myself elevated wishful thinking to a whole new realm of magical reconstructions of reality. I was a most helpless, overwhelmed and anxiously lost leader of a one-man expedition. It did not help when some frustrated comedian ran over to me in mock panic and said: "Where are your parents?" When I stood there in stunned silence, he followed with: "Oh, I thought your parents forgot you when they dropped off your older sibling." The "mistake" was understandable. Delayed adolescence is a neuroendocrine malady that left me developmentally delayed, looking and sounding like prepubescent until oral testosterone kick-started my adolescence in my 18th year. Even then my emotional age still lagged behind my biological age, as evidenced by my reaction to my first masturbatory orgasm.

Immediately after the initial shock of this bone-jarring experience, I ran into the dorm suite of an older friend and announced I had just completed my first successful orgasm, as if expecting him to share my pride and joy, as might an older brother. My floor mate was boundlessly amused by my ebullience and equally kind so as not to humiliate me in a moment of great vulnerability.

SUNY Binghamton was approximately 200 miles from my home in Brooklyn, yet judging by the near state of panic expressed in unison by the brain cells of my gastrointestinal tract, one might have imagined I had been dropped by helicopter some 2,000 miles away in some South American rain forest minus survival gear. Yes, there are many colleagues of mine these days that believe that our "gut" is a satellite brain with its own memory storage system sometimes in communication with the brain inside our skulls. In my case its SOS signals were indecipherable and unanswered by my other brain, which was equally under siege by excess neural stimulation.

Needless to say, I felt stressed out and depressed about being stressed out and depressed, as no one in my natal family dignified my adjustment as understandably difficult. I was mortified at not having the energy or motivation to hide my naked grief, as I secretly hoped someone would claim me and care for me the way that a rescue dog might be fortunate enough to find a home. It was sheer lunacy, born of purely wishful thinking, that I would go away to college and make my parents proud. If not for the good-humored and good-natured sympathy of upperclassmen on my floor who had weathered similar bouts of homesickness, I might have well "cried uncle" and returned home.

In truth, my gritty determination to gut it out and make college my home was rooted in my desperation to wean myself off of my mother's rather dried-up breasts. I could not bear to be in her midst while at college, as her worries were contagious and would have only made matters worse for me. With me out of sight, my mother's obsessive worries about me were out of mind. At least they were not on my radar to activate my internal mother who hovered over me with worry and left me amnestic about being 18 and so instead treated me as if I were eight.

For her part, my mother worked to fill the void left by my departure. Mom, to her credit, found a more adaptive transitional object than myself, in a manner of speaking. She joined a sister program of AA known as Overeaters Anonymous. Ruth was now ready to let go of her son whom she no longer needed to function as a container for her disavowed and disowned insecurities. For my mother, living with my emotionally disconnected and insensitive father was very much like living alone.

I had been her little co-conspirator, acting out on my mother's behalf her guilty desires to oppose and defy my father's obnoxious patriarchal ways. I was her emotional confidant and an emotionally incestuous love object. Now Mom had the support of an entire fellowship group. She had gained control of the self-destructive eating that had been her primary means to lick wounds of neglect and abuse inflicted on her. Unfortunately Mom's newfound sobriety from overeating was short-lived. Dad's fears that Mom's growing self-esteem would result in an exit strategy from their failed marriage was so contagious that when he encouraged her to resume her old eating habits, she took him up on it.

At school, my roommate was very kind, patient and compassionate with me, despite doing my best impression of a hypochondriac sitting with his internist reviewing his recent medical history. My gastrointestinal system cried bloody murder for a solid six months straight while I tried to adapt to a quantum leap in personal responsibility.

Eventually, what did not kill me made me realize I was stronger and more adaptive than I had ever considered. The evidence raised my head above my own clouds of panic and some time in

February 1973, as "Crocodile Rock" blared from my clock radio, I stopped holding my breath, bracing for some nebulous disaster. The brain in my gut had rejected most if not all nourishment up until that point, as if I were the recipient of an organ transplant my immune system was treating as a foreign agent. I see now as a historical observer how food symbolized emotional nourishment, and how what my mother had fed me all these years left me unfit to survive on my own.

Once maintaining my balance in the wake of these emotional shockwaves did not consume so much of my time and energy, the thought unknown to me was: "Never again would I risk loving anyone and needing them so that to lose them would be a personal catastrophe." I decided to be my own island of serenity. This turned my attentions inward, making myself an object of a budding affair of self-love. Even if I had read the myth of Narcissus, I doubt its ominous message would have penetrated my denial. The stage was set for me falling head over heels for some drug of choice. Though the acute symptoms of homesickness subsided, I would be dishonest to tell you that my gastrointestinal problems disappeared entirely. I continued to ingest too many unhealthy, somewhat indigestible calories, and did not exercise sufficiently to discharge the nervous energies dysregulating my digestive and eliminatory processes.

Being perhaps one of the worst college golfers in NCAA Division III history only left me enviously alienated from my male peers. Looking at myself in the mirror, it was hard to debate the sarcastic critics of golfers as not deserving to be called athletes. Due to the influx of oral testosterone, I was growing, but I was soft, weak, slow afoot, and lacking endurance. So, I took a gym class titled "Running to Awareness."

The instructor of "Running to Awareness" was SUNY Binghamton Men's Track & Field Coach, Dr. Gary Truce. We still meet for breakfast on occasion when I travel to Ithaca to visit my younger daughter. My desire for this idealized man to offer me the praise and admiration withheld by my father and brother led me to sign on as the track team's manager. Soon I was traveling with the team and working out with them every afternoon. Like magic, the excess energies that had previously instigated my painful gastric preoccupations were no more.

I ceased to be my father's embarrassing twin worried about the constipation, painful flatulence, and diarrhea that compelled me to leave lectures midstream. Running required that I not eat three to four hours before exercising. My new active lifestyle was not conducive to eating the fatty, hard-to-digest foods that would be a drag on my system while exercising. So, my diet improved and the synergistic effect of eating better, eating less, and exercising regularly left me shorn of the baby fat-laden, wide-hipped feminine look that had promoted an identification with my mother and had left me feeling like an emotional hermaphrodite.

It was not long before I looked like every other beanpole of a male college student. My sense of not being man enough to belong among the guys became invisible to the naked eye. For the most part I was able to repress my anxieties over years of being bullied and humiliated for being short, weak, fearful, and needy. My homophobic paranoia fueled by fears that my desire for male affection would be mistaken for homosexual desire, evaporated. They were replaced by a narcissistic love for equating my newfound athleticism with my perfectionistic ego ideal. I might not have shined on the basketball court, coed gridiron, or tennis court. However, I was fast earning respect as a runner. Heck, it helped my reputation that many on campus mistook me as a varsity member of the cross-country team. I enjoyed an image of false modesty covering up exhibitionistic desires to dance on the graves of those who had humiliated me with their superior physical strength and courage. I imagined vanquishing them all in an endurance contest on the roads. Massive denial of my rage-fueled envy allowed for superficial friendliness towards the other jocks on campus. Who needed their respect and admiration when I could claim as running buddies some of their favorite professors? Yes, I was not yet advanced enough to run with my peers, but I was well suited to keep pace with middle-aged running junkies losing metabolic battles with their own midriff bulges.

For my running-companion professors and myself, these shared experiences of struggle with the limits of our physical endurance and mental fatigue were great social levelers. To fart, sweat, breathe heavily, expel mucous, and spit in efforts to self-regulate as our bodies adapted to the stresses and strains of distance running were precious bonding experiences. Even though these men were almost old enough to be my fathers, out on the roads we were intimates who shared private concerns. It was like being a member of a therapy group. We might not be comfortable together in a social setting, yet on the roads we were comrades in arms. I found myself philosophizing about matters I knew very little about, such as love and sex, never realizing until this moment how much I was speaking out of my hat and so much like my father in this regard.

Running became my mistress. I felt like a million bucks courting her daily, and after a workout I was immediately okay with a universe I ordinarily regarded with suspicion and skepticism. Being high on endorphins and dopamine left me feeling like a beloved celebrity. It did not cross my mind to consider that my crazed fan club numbered one member. It was so easy early on to regularly establish new personal bests for distance and time runs. These novel achievements were rewarded by a fresh infusion of feel-good hormones. I was exploring individual frontiers in strength and endurance. At the ends of my workouts I was in my mind's eye every bit as resourceful, intrepid, strong, and undaunted as mountain climber Edmund Hillary, frontiersman Davey Crockett, and intergalactic peacekeeper, James T. Kirk. As I started slipping into the rhythm of workouts, it was easy early on to overlook how much a slave I was becoming to my routines.

Catch me for the first few hours after a run and I was the relaxed, open, friendly, and confident guy you would put at the top of your party invitation list. My lingering runner's high was the equivalent of some alcoholic student's beer bottle that appeared to be a natural extension of his arm. But if I had not worked out earlier in the day, I was not long for any party and made myself as inconspicuous as was humanly possible. Even if I had run, as the evenings wore on and I dried out on dopamine, a very palpable belittling sensation reemerged into my consciousness. I was typically long gone from these parties by the time students "hooked up" and continued their reveling in private. By the time the clock struck 11:00 PM on a Saturday evening I did my best impression of a male Cinderella beating my retreat to my dorm room before I turned into a pumpkin.

While I physically began to look the part of a college student, I still felt like an impostor of a love object to any adolescent young woman. Even having crested the puberty hump and now in possession of the goods to perform in bed, I felt about as potent as I might have felt emerging from a long bath as a child with my father drawing derisive attention to my small and shriveled phallus.

Instead of engaging in adolescent rites of courtship, I poured my passion into running until the pursuit of my daily fix resulted in inflammation of my right hip that sidelined me shortly before graduation. I had come to live for the joy of running, and without this activity I entered a dark, miserable tunnel. There had been a time in the not so distant past when a teacher's approving smile, a friend's party invitation or a sympathetic ear could repair my alienation from a world that seemed to mock me as recreation. Now this wounded hip was my badge of shameful weakness, and any attention I received felt like the laser-glare of the sun on an over exposed and inflamed patch of skin.

If I had instead at this point in my life been able to observe and think about my self-pity, I would have heard my father's dirges over his aching back. Dad's aching back had been an all-purpose excuse for opting out of fatherly responsibilities like playing catch with me, taking an interest in my school work or helping me lick my wounds when performance anxieties on my fields of dreams got the best of me. Like Dad, now my complaints were thinly veiled demands for someone to make me feel better or go away and leave me alone. I had nothing to give them for their time and trouble, and resented feeling obligated to thank them for their interest. Why did they deserve to enjoy themselves while I was suffering so?

While my fellow students, in eager anticipation of graduation, staged their own jubilant versions of music videos befitting a Beach Boys record, I walked miles outside of campus to simulate a work-out and burn calories. I had become a slave to exercise. Addiction has a way of turning conscious beings into Pavlov-like, behaviorally conditioned dogs. Now stripped of running, I found myself desperately trying to shore the dam against my growing emotional hunger. The battleground shifted to my caloric intake.

I was apt to hate myself as much as my father hated himself, and my mother and me, for indulging our appetites for food. I was not running and therefore not burning large sums of calories, so I would not under any circumstances yield to hunger outside the prescribed "stuffing my face" sessions at breakfast and dinner. Remaining rail thin was now a huge challenge, as it took many more hours of walking to burn an equal number of calories one would burn running five to eight miles. With my course load, this was an impossible feat. If I gave into being human I chastised myself—as Dad would have had he not been 200 miles away.

I longed for caring human contact but denied it at all costs. I would have risked dying of loneliness at the hands of my empty reflection in the mirror than to need others and then risk those dreaded withdrawal symptoms associated with loss and separation.

There was not anything inherently repulsive about me. I had simply no idea how to care for myself, let alone anyone else, and tossed away any gifts of caring extended toward me. I covered all bases, ensuring that no one would make me important, because I did not have a clue what it meant to make them important.

As crazy as this sounds, it sounded reasonable to me coming from a perspective of wishing to ward off loss at all costs. In my warped and contracted addictive mind, my self-esteem was rooted in one metric: Did I gain or not gain weight? While I could not be the intrepid explorer on asphalt, I could be special by virtue of establishing omnipotent control over my caloric needs. What kept me going despite being bored out of my mind was the hope that my hip would heal so that I could once again see the sun up in the sky.

That summer an orthopedist diagnosed me as having a "tired" hip. I rested for a few weeks and when I returned to running, I felt like I had a new lease on life. Still, on occasion I could not avoid flashes of insight into my enslavement to this activity. For example, one early July evening my best friend Phil, home on summer leave from the University of Florida, invited me to a party. I had been busy that day and did not have time to work out prior to his invitation. My personality had become so rigid that I declined the party in favor of a workout. My angst was excruciating, as I sorely wanted to experience the sexual tension between myself and other attractive young women. But Phil was not going to be late for the party, so I could feed my neurosis.

Phil looked incredulously at me, as if he intuited how lonely I truly was and how irrational was my retreat from this night out. He then disparaged me with stifled mock laughter. I had no idea, and most definitely neither did Phil, that my staying behind was in part taking displaced revenge on my father and to a lesser degree my brother for rejecting my desire to be with them when that interest was not mutual. I had no capacity for empathy for Phil that evening, and the manner in which Phil communicated his hurt feelings validated my belief that I was best served not needing anyone.

Let's fast forward to 1978, when at the height of the running boom I lived within three-quarters of a mile of Central Park. Frederick Law Olmsted's garden jewel had become the mecca for everyone who found it fashionable in their leisure time to rediscover or perhaps discover for the very first time their inner athletes. Business women and men used endurance events as training grounds to fuel their competitive drives and build self-confidence to prove that they had the "right stuff." It was the perfect environment for my addiction to progress.

Since I was qualified to do absolutely nothing of a skilled nature after dropping out of law school, I gravitated to the job listings that were titled: "College graduates: No experience necessary." I landed a job as a technical recruiter for an employment agency. "Technical recruiter" was a fancy term for cold canvassing, telephone sales. On the skilled employment food chain we garnered the respect accorded white-collar scavengers. My office was divided into two categories. In the blue corner of the boiler-room-like ring were those without formal education, unskilled anti-establishment types who looked to make a fast, unscrupulous buck. In the red corner sat the educated, skilled employees in engineering fields who led undistinguished careers playing the establishment game and who now hoped in loosening their ties both figuratively and literally to sacrifice some integrity to cash in on the computer age while sounding and looking more dignified than their crass colleagues. They lorded their technical acumen over their rough and rugged counterparts, and yet, in most cases the "street crowd" had a much better knack for making money. Nothing got in the way of throwing job candidates against the walls of their corporate clients to see who would stick. This was a sales job, pure and simple, which required thick skin, an aggressive, engaging and energetic personality, and a conscience filled with holes like Swiss cheese.

I was an odd bird here. I was educated in the humanities, was not street wise, and had been asked to find jobs for computer hardware technicians, a field about which I knew nothing. Curiously, my unheralded survivor instincts kicked in. I compensated for my thin skin by faking it. I was a hard worker like my father and felt a kinship to him engaged in a rather uninteresting job that compelled me to prostitute my dignity and worth. Soliciting job leads could be as discouraging as trying to get a date by randomly calling female names in the phone book. On some days my success rate was no better.

Taken as a whole, the job was perfect for me. I was a man on the mission to not let anything interfere with my training regimen, including matters of conscience. Somehow I earned my keep and was able to pay the modest rent for my studio apartment. And no matter what was happening at work, at 6:00 PM I managed to rendezvous with the herds of runners who met at 90th Street and Fifth Avenue for group workouts. The neurochemical alterations to my brain produced by running left me feeling as if I had accomplished great things in this world for doing nothing more than diligently preparing to break three hours for the marathon.

Improvements came fast and furious in the beginning and if my times did not always reflect it, I felt like a million bucks after an endorphin-drenched long run. You have heard of the condition known as "lazy eye." Well, addicts develop lazy brains. I became careless and carefree as my life progressively revolved around the enjoyment of and recovery from the euphoria I lived for. My attachments to more moderate forms of pleasure went the way of train tracks no longer in use, overgrown with weeds. I was in total denial that my artificially engineered identity was a house of cards that if blown on the wrong way would collapse. All I knew was that by increasing my mileage in pursuit of lowering my marathon time, my brain's pharmacy kept dispensing feel-good drugs. It was like playing with house money at a casino, confident that those one-arm bandits would dispense gloriously predictable thrills. I conducted my life as if I were an Olympic hopeful. Unfortunately, world-class marathoners are born before they are made. You cannot teach world-class speed no matter the race distance, and I was not born to rip off 26 consecutive miles in under five minutes. Yet, I would not let the truth get in the way of a delightful dream. As long as the limits of my potential were very much an unknown, I was able to insert my fantasies into the vacuum of facts. My default rationalization for permitting running to consume my life was that I might qualify to coach world-class runners one day if I could not be one.

Working for a living helped structure my days, but if you asked me, my real job was running. My training progressed from 30-40, to 60-75 miles per week, and as the 1978 New York City Marathon approached, I was too tired to care much about anything including balancing checkbooks, organizing my files, dating, paying electricity and rent, or attending conscientiously to my work duties. The conscious fiction that helped regulate my self-esteem was that if I were not so busy with more important matters (i.e., running), then I would manage these affairs willingly and competently with a minimum of performance anxieties. My actions were indefensible but my executive functions had so atrophied that I was unaware of the poor mental shape I was in. My defenses against my shrinking capacities to safeguard my health and welfare meant that I required a growing cast of characters to protect me from consequences of my impulsive neglect and abuse of my body. Without others' willingness to compensate for my growing deficits by covering for me and enabling my impulse control disorder, I could not have continued this insanity. My main posse of "yes men" consisted of the aforementioned "colleagues" at work who were as equally allergic to being told "no" as myself, since they, too, were legends in their own minds who politely said "Excuse me" before pushing you out of their way. So, one hand washed another. My other handlers were a group of my running peers who like me were totally consumed by their obsessions with distance running. There was nothing wrong with me because when they looked at me they saw themselves, and there could not possibly be anything wrong with them and their obsessions with and compulsions for running.

My fellow runners were monotonous and tedious to relate to. Did they really think during our runs that anyone other than their mothers wanted to know what they had eaten from the time they arose in the morning? Okay, maybe it was my envy for their patience with keeping records of training miles and caloric intake that made them seem insufferable. Or maybe it was the fact that, unlike myself, some of my road companions had careers, close friends, lovers, and enough disposable income to indulge desires to vacation and pursue other hobbies. I, on the other hand, was a one-trick pony with a one-track mind.

I lived for the feeling of flow produced by my success synchronizing my breathing to the rhythms of my footfalls. My body's intelligence about the physics of achieving and maintaining momentum was so gratifying that I figured the lighter and narrower I was, the less wind and air resistance would slow me down. Most of my male counterparts were fighting a never-ending, and in many cases, losing battle with a bottomless pit of hunger that spurred them to keep eating. No matter how many thousands of calories my guy friends burned on the roads, they somehow managed to be overweight, quite a feat of thermodynamics, their girth somehow a statement of their male power. They wore their guts as medals of prosperity.

I speculated that over-eating became a means of self-soothing their anxieties and fears about being (or not) top dogs in their packs. Many ran 60-80 miles per week to keep up with their competition and to keep up with their growing caloric intakes. Part of what it meant to have the "right stuff" on the roads and in life was to gut it out, despite gorging one's self with food and alcohol. It may be hard to imagine that anyone could run 70-85 miles per week and be 15 pounds overweight. One old buddy John would eat an entire Entenmann's chocolate cream filled crumb cake (at least he had good taste in junk food) before joining me on a quick eight-mile run in Central Park. That's enough calories to meet someone's energy requirements for a day or more. How he managed not to barf it all up is something I still marvel at.

During my short stint coaching female distance runners, I recall one of my athletes telling me with a straight face after a 20-mile run that she was going to walk home to Greenwich Village from Central Park. It was a miracle of self-restraint to keep the shock from my face. She would not be dissuaded. This Olympic Trials hopeful was on the stocky side. Others of us could have been the poster children for campaigns fighting world hunger, and yet when we looked in the mirror we still saw with contempt and disgust, "fat."

I can poke fun at these folks' foibles all I want and yet the sad truth was that their lives were far more balanced than mine. It is a lot easier to go off the deep end if you have less to lose and fewer people to hurt. That pretty well sums me up in the late 1970s. I had very little to keep my addiction in check. I looked not by accident more like some waif-like woman or prepubescent child, anything to stave off the fat jokes still echoing in my dreams. My motto was that if I could not make the Fortune 500 list of the well-to-do, then maybe I could rise to the top as a marathoner.

I still identified with my father humiliating me as a child for being like my mother—weak and vulnerable, insatiable, out of control, and helplessly infantile. My mission was to prove Dad wrong while distancing myself from identification with my embarrassing and shameful mother who got so big at one point that if you stuck her with a pin, she might burst. I will admit now that wasting away

31

was delightfully cruel and sadistic, as Dad was quite pained to watch me literally eat myself alive to compensate for my neglected caloric needs. I doubt my father ever considered this was my way of taking revenge on him for leaving me so painfully self-conscious over my former obesity. What was so unsympathetically cruel and sadistic about my calorie restrictions in the late 1970s was that I must have reminded my father of the concentration camp survivors inside Germany he liberated and had the responsibility as a cook to nurture back to health. They were barely more than skin-covered skeletons, and here I was, his little shit, bringing him back to these horrific images of human beings treated like stray animals. I am dearly sorry, Dad. Two wrongs did not make a right.

When I weighed myself an hour or so after completing the 1978 New York City Marathon, I was a very self-satisfied 122 pounds and happy to feel deserving of a large dinner. My skeletal likeness effectively kept women away who I feared would reject me for being too child-like, or too feminine in my sensibilities. My inevitable comparisons to more balanced running partners left me feeling wanting and meanwhile comfortably unaware of how I was beating myself up over perceived relative inadequacies. Starvation, was my desperate foothold for a vaunted superiority over these guys. They were "obviously" undisciplined and weak in being so overly self-indulgent as to allow themselves to carry so much weight while racing. How seriously could they take themselves, investing all this time in training only to sabotage their performance with weight? Restricting my calories and skipping lunch became my badge of gritty determination to succeed.

Typically I permitted myself two soft-boiled eggs, a roll and coffee in the morning, followed by a cup of Dannon vanilla yogurt and a banana at lunchtime. This diet would not meet the fuel requirements of our 100-pound secretary who complained about the exertion of having to walk from her reception desk back to our sales desks (her exercise for the day).

The fatigue of running more miles than my body could reasonably recover from in 24 hours was exacerbated by my chronic low blood sugar. It was as if I felt forced to starve myself to create an involuntary state of irritability, when the ulterior motive behind my less than sunny disposition was to get away with murder, girded by a sense of entitlement to "act out" and displace grudges and grievances toward my father onto my supervisor, Dick. In essence, I was speaking to my father saying, "Don't you dare tell me what to do after years of abdicating your fiduciary duty to raise me to be a man and then put me down when I gravitated to my mother for guidance and nurturance!" "Leave me the hell alone. You asked for this!"

The last thing in truth was that Dick asked for it. He surely did not deal well with my biting irritability when he dared ask me what I was doing with my time. Tired, hungry, and irritable, I walked around as if I did not care about anything. If I were hungry and mildly irritable by 10:30 AM, the afternoons were much worse. Curiously Dick was intimidated by my rather mindlessly oppositional nature. Were there thoughts unknown to my conscious mind that my boss was vulnerable to being intimidated by my terse and begrudging responses? My best guess was that when he could not humorously point out that he was not my father, he kept his distance as if the more he became irritated with me the more he became afraid of his own anger and the more he associated such internal tensions to walking on eggshells with his alcoholic father. This was to my great advantage, as my inner biological tensions made it difficult to do my job.

Starving myself became such a problem that I developed gastritis, which as I understand it is an irritation of the abdominal lining caused by secretions of gastric enzymes in an empty stomach. I did not cause serious harm to myself. However, the acute symptoms of these flare-ups felt as if a gang of hoods had kicked me hard in the stomach and my only relief was to lie on my belly.

Between meals my stomach was apt to spasm with cramps, and most foods when ingested had an identical effect. Sadly, despite my doctor's admonishment about restricting calories, my first priority remained to not gain weight. My valued self-image was supported by two dysfunctional pillars—training and starving—that intertwined like strands of DNA forming a double helix. Together they defined me as strong, self-sufficient and Spartan.

The interesting thing about restricting calories was that sometimes late in the afternoon, close to the end of the business day, I would get beyond being hungry and feel as relaxed and content as if I had a meal, a nap and a massage. Short of that threshold, my behavior became shameless to the point of being antisocial. I would do or say anything to not be waylaid from meeting my running group. My panic and worry was so contagious and unsettling that even though everyone in the office had me pegged as fibbing to get my way, they all momentarily froze, caught up in reliving with me desperate enactments of my own past. I became very powerful manipulating others to rescue me from responsibility for my artificially manufactured crises. As addiction eroded my abilities to manage adult responsibilities, my world shrunk accordingly. I ate, slept, worked out, raced, went through the motions at work, and when I could fit it in, did laundry and cleaned my apartment. The highlight of my Saturday evenings was to walk to First Avenue and East 79th Street to buy the Sunday New York Times. I hoped not be seen by peers walking alone. I kept company on Saturday nights with "Saturday Night with Sinatra," a popular radio show of that era on WYNY. Upon returning home paper in hand, I tuned in.

The wheels abruptly came off my addictive bus in 1978. For some time, both knees had been aching between workouts. While training in Central Park in preparation for my third marathon in two months (yes, you heard this insanity correctly), the tendons in my right knee echoed Roberto Duran's notorious declaration of defeat: "No mas." I went from running 75 miles a week saturated in dopamine and endorphins and feeling little or no emotional or physical pain, to limping around horribly depressed. Even with the wheels coming off the bus of addiction, I kept trying to drive that bus for weeks, months and years until limping around became so habitual that even when I finally healed up, I limped out of habit. Trying to run, despite having difficulties walking, resulted in a string of nagging muscular and connective tissue injuries.

I hit bottom around the time of the 1980 Winter Olympics in Lake Placid. Sidelined from running with chronic injuries and un-employed by virtue of having finally been fired from my recruiting job for insubordination, I was desperate enough to ask for help in spite of my distrust of people. My next-door neighbor, Lynn, suggested I speak with a psychotherapist who engaged her as a personal fitness instructor. Sometime in early 1981, Dr. G and I embarked together on a very bumpy road to recovery.

Running had been an addictive mask covering the insecurities and compulsions created by early trauma. Now, without running, it was time to look these traumas in the eye.

CHAPTER 4

DISABILITY IS IN THE MIND OF THE BEHOLDER:
THE LIFE AND TIMES OF NAOMI DAVISON
(NOVEMBER 11, 1925 – MARCH 3, 1989)

Perched on the dresser of my Aunt Naomi's bedroom, the same small bedroom once occupied by my maternal grandparents was a picture of a youthful, wholesomely beautiful and healthy young woman flashing a radiant smile. The smile was high-octane fuel for my spirit. If you saw this picture of my aunt at age 16 and then met Naomi for the first time 20 years later, you would swear that the ingénue in the frame could not be the person in front of you. This chapter is her story, my mother's kid sister who stood out from my parents' families like a proud peacock amidst bloodlines whose damaged and lackluster feathers told stories of shameless internecine warfare. Early on I did not appreciate Naomi's intuitive genius for making her grateful best of the moment. Today, I reverently understand that most everything I needed to know about successful living sat in her Everest Jennings wheelchair.

Rheumatoid arthritis is a chronic inflammatory disorder that typically affects the small joints in your hands and feet. Unlike the wear-and-tear of osteoarthritis, rheumatoid arthritis affects the lining of your joints. It causes a painful swelling that may eventually lead to bone erosion and joint deformity. As is the nature of auto-immune disorders, the immune system mistakenly attacks one's own tissues. In addition to causing joint problems, rheumatoid arthritis may affect other organs of the body—such as the skin, eyes, lungs, and blood vessels.

Rheumatoid arthritis is a bit like having your body under siege by a guerilla insurgency; an insurgency bent on destroying your biological infrastructure of systems of regulation, growth, and repair. Rheumatoid arthritis holds the potential to break the human spirit by wreaking physiological mayhem. This chronic illness is notorious for leaving its victims helplessly dejected and demoralized. Naomi was no one or no-thing's victim. If you asked, she would not hesitate to set the record straight. My heroic aunt withstood this illness's thundering body blows, shook them off and kept moving forward. She reminds me of the great middleweight champion Marvin Hagler. However, Naomi did not know Marvin Hagler from Marvin Greenstein who owned the local butcher shop.

My research in preparation for writing this memoir casts doubt about the accuracy of Naomi's diagnosis conveyed to me during my childhood. I am left wondering if her condition was more likely psoriatic arthritis, an illness that includes a skin condition commonly known as psoriasis. Apart from my aunt's red plaque-like patches of skin on her legs and arms, she also exhibited symptoms of both arthritis mutilans (a long-term form of destructive psoriatic arthritis in which the joints are severely damaged and deformities can be seen, especially in the hands and feet) and spondylitis (inflammation of the vertebrae in the spine with inflammation of the sacroiliac joint in the pelvis). Any way you slice it, my aunt was royally screwed.

To the best of my knowledge, there were no effective treatments for rheumatoid arthritis during my aunt's lifetime. She waged a daily battle for survival against pain, which, judging by how much she clenched her jaw and shook with muscular fatigue from spasms of tension, wandered on a pain meter between a numerical score of 6 to 12, on a scale from 1 to 10.

If you personified rheumatoid arthritis, it would be a conscience-less sociopath, possessed of the indefatigable and maniacal passion of a suicide bomber bent on fomenting chaos and bringing any challengers to the hegemony of their dogma to their knees. Without mercy it did its devil's work on my aunt at a torturously slow pace. The pièce de résistance of her affliction was the agonizing attacks on the nerves in her spine.

Although her universe was admittedly stupefied by her grit, self-pity was not a word in my aunt's vocabulary. It was as unlikely to find her in bed during the day as one might find a farmer in bed after sunrise during harvest season or a city snow plow driver in bed after a fresh snow. Naomi had vials of untouched prescription pain medications in a medicine cabinet that was a junkie's paradise. My aunt dared not compromise her mental acuity. She had a house to manage. I believe these vials of expired medications sat there to collect dust as an affirmation of her determination to battle this disease to the bitter end. They were the only objects in an apartment that did not meet some military standard of order and cleanliness. When I say you could eat off of the linoleum floors, I mean it literally. Naomi stopped at nothing to defeat her interminable foes, dust and grime. Picture for a moment if you will my wheelchair-bound aunt with no seat belt or safety harness bent over like a collapsed folding chair to clean some inaccessible nook and cranny of a section of her bathroom floor. She would have been the envy of a professional contortionist engaged in such a maneuver.

When she was not up and about during the day, something was terribly wrong. This was the era of doctor house calls and when rheumatoid arthritis staged an uprising in or around my aunt's spinal column, she would lie in bed screaming in agony as if she were a POW being tortured, waiting for her rheumatologist, Dr.

Constance, to arrive for an emergency visit. Every few minutes, her body stiffened as if electric shocks coursed through her body. Once on the scene, Dr. Constance injected an opioid and was on his way. Only then did Naomi's spasms subside and she fell asleep, exhausted from the energy expended to accommodate the demands of a system wracked by muscular spasms.

The next morning it was business as usual. She had a house to run, loved ones to take care of and support, and an attorney to perform administrative duties for. Life was about her meaningful devotion to serving others. To paraphrase Carly Simon, she didn't have time for the pain.

The damage inflicted by chronic arthritis on her body over time was staggering. What Naomi could not use, she lost use of forever. This reality terrified me because when I was overly anxious, I felt as if significant portions of my brain were also lost forever. By the time my aunt was in her early thirties, she was paralyzed from the waist down and confined to a wheelchair. Her legs became lifeless twigs. The terrain of her body was pockmarked with open sores. Her eye sockets were dark sunken hollows, probably a symptom of chronic restlessness at night. She progressively lost the use of her hands as her body cannibalized her finger joints and her fingers shrunk. So my aunt, challenged to comb her own hair, kept it very short, exposing rather humorously large elephantine ears. She was quick to joke about her appearance as if to make light of her losses. I was ever so careful during the writing of this tribute not to confuse sympathy with pity. One did not pity Naomi if she was within earshot. If you catch my historical drift, such a communication was an act of infamy for this FDR groupie. If you are listening Aunt Naomi, no offense intended.

To love this woman the way she required you to love her, you did not dare think to yourself even in private that she possessed a weak or vulnerable mental bone in her body. Such was unthinkable. No one intimated in the most delicate manner that this warrior in a decades-long war with rheumatoid arthritis might let her guard down for even one second. We knew implicitly, if not explicitly, that Naomi was terrified to lay down her character armor for more than the time it took to drink a cup of coffee and smoke an unfiltered Camel cigarette. What might happen to her remained an unprocessed idea in her dynamic unconscious life.

I am inclined these days to interpret my aunt's fearlessness as her emotional numbing to trauma. Rheumatoid arthritis precipitated an identity crisis of horrific proportions. Yet, it is my contention now that Naomi became numb much earlier in life to protect herself from the emotional contagion that were my grandparents' hard-to-contain, life-and-death dramas of persecution growing up as Jews in Czarist Russia. These subversive and un-integrated flashbacks that annihilated the boundaries of time were as much an emotional menace as the disease was a physical menace.

This is probably why Naomi was bulletproof while listening to me emote. This theory also explains why my aunt kept her distance from and ignored my reports of being bullied by my peers. I learned to not expect any more help from Naomi in dealing with these matters than was offered by my parents. What remained a thought unknown during my childhood was that had Naomi stuck her nose in my affairs, my parents might have felt criticized or judged and pulled the plug on our frequent visits. I dared not risk losing Naomi's love.

Naomi did not fret over how rheumatoid arthritis would eventually cannibalize her and render her incapable of executing activities of daily living. This looming dark cloud must have fortified the household's denial that Chuck's alcoholism had him heading for terminal problems. My uncle, and my aunt, held fast to his self-image as the able-bodied, indestructible white knight. Meanwhile, as the designated repository holding every vestige of arrested development for both of them, he had her green light to drown his sorrows over a childhood shorn of carefree pleasures afforded children with a male breadwinner in residence. Chuck's father did his best Harry Houdini impression, and Chuck was prematurely pressed into service as a household wage earner. Chuck, to his developmental misfortune, was conscripted by his mother to be her "little man" and fill the void left by his father. After his mother died, Chuck remained my aunt's "little man" by dint of alcohol's destructive impact on his inchoate potential to become the adult in charge of his now grown-up body. He remained until his death a child frozen in time inside a once muscular and now deteriorating body.

Aunt Naomi managed the household, her illness, and Chuck's basic needs. She smoked unfiltered Camel cigarettes, in part to relieve the stress of emotional needs unmet by her husband.

To me, this small depressed boy vexed by psychosomatic stomach pains who was frightfully convinced were misdiagnosed symptoms of terminal cancer, my aunt's aloof attitude about death was quite alien. In "The Denial of Death," Ernest Becker offers a model that helped me understand how my aunt coped with the death of her healthy body, once a deep reservoir of narcissistic pride. As necessity is often the mother of invention, Naomi identified with a God-like mind she called "me" and dis-identified with her diseased and decaying body that became "not me." The evidence that this God-like mind could not exist without her body and vice versa did not temper her steadfast illusion.

My aunt was a paradox. On a physical level she was as defenseless against aggressors as I was emotionally as a child. Yet emotionally she owned more phallic power than all three male members of my family combined. She was as impenetrable as the fortress-like perimeter around Fort Knox. One did not sooner slight my aunt than one might eagerly pose a threat to a paranoid megalomaniac tyrant in possession of a nuclear arsenal. During my childhood, her will appeared as indomitable as an earthquake, her reservoir of self-confidence as deep as the ocean, and her self-esteem was as resilient as a rubber ball being pitched to a hitter wielding a plastic whiffle ball bat. The image of my aunt's diseased legs surrounding the portal to the miracle that is a woman's reproductive organs percolated in my psyche. I, too, had become paralyzed as a compromise between needing my early attachment figures to care for me, and fearing that they would violate and traumatize me.

If not for Naomi modeling a penis-less identity as a powerful, competent and respected figure, I might have become depressed beyond help over having been born male to a father who wanted a daughter. At best, my penis represented a symbol of my truncated, slow to develop, and fragile male power. At worst, there were times during my childhood I felt like an emotional hermaphrodite and seriously wondered if I had been screwed being born as an anatomical male. It seemed growing up that everyone owned my penis except me.

As a mother-like martyr of a child, my male peers salivated at the sight of me, and they used me like a rag doll. Mama and papa mammals do not typically kill off their young. However, I felt all bets were off outside my home. I was acutely aware of having a bull's eye on my back for peers who were victims of childhood abuse and out to take revenge on the weak and vulnerable they were taught deserved to be bullied. I was easy prey. On one hand I was terrified of my own aggression should it boomerang in a flurry of fists. Therefore I did not show my "aggressive hand" and fight back when accosted. On the other, I was too slow a foot to evade my would-be predators. If you added a dash of my homophobia to the mix for good measure, then you understand that no matter how bad I had it at home, I was not about to leave the fold and try and survive in the urban jungle.

My gender identity and my sexual identity were so mired in conflict that had the wind blown differently during pivotal developmental periods, I might have fallen off the fence and landed firmly on the ground as a homosexual transvestite.

If my aunt ever knew me, she knew me only as she needed me to be. Thus we maintained a fluid narcissistic relationship. We believed we knew what the other needed based on our own regulatory needs. This worked fine for me as long as I had an idealized other whose perfection compensated for all my imperfections, and alternately whose blind adoration obfuscated my warts. This towering figure of strength offered me her apartment as a refuge from the emotional torments being bullied by my parents and peers. She was so calm and reassuring that I bought into the notion that she knew something about my future I was not privy to. I wanted to believe Naomi was clairvoyant and foresaw that one day, removed from the toxic environment of my parents' home, I would transcend my emotional traumas the way she transcended her physical traumas.

I hope you will give me the benefit of the doubt when I say there was at minimum a dotted-line relationship between debts of gratitude and debts of survivor guilt over being able bodied, and the birth of my love affair with running. If my aunt could train her mind to be indestructible in spite of the unending threat posed by her physical trauma, then maybe I could train my legs to be indestructible and one day they could become my guardian angels to carry me out of harm's way, either kicking my tormentors away, outrunning them, or perhaps turning the tables and making one of them the fall guy for past crimes committed against me by an entire class of bullies. I chuckle as I write this because I never did and probably never will prove my mettle in hand-to-hand combat. Even today I would not dare risk getting my face handed to me or alternately, winding up in jail. My best bet to defend this bona fide "sissy boy" at heart may forever rest with me training the larger muscles of my legs and hips. Maybe my time-honored belief is that my legs may cast long enough shadows over a castrated phallus to protect it from exposure to hostile forces. Early on, in fact for most of my life until recent times, my contempt and hatred for my weaknesses and vulnerabilities made it very hard for me to imagine any guy treating me with compassion and sympathy, let alone respect.

To some degree I was off the hook until I reached puberty, when my excuses for being impotent would expire. Freud said that sometimes a cigar is a cigar and not a symbolic representation of a penis. Well, for five years from age 13 until 18, I walked around swinging golf clubs with the regularity of an elephant swinging its trunk. Until I had my head examined, I had no idea why swinging these clubs in a full arc at a little ball in full view of others left me so anxious. It was as if I were walking around naked wishing to exhibit my penis for the admiration and praise of others, while meanwhile I wished to smash down the fairway these symbolic representations of the testicles of more powerful males I hatefully envied. These wishful gratifications are ones I may never cease to enjoy.

I have already laid out for you that golf for me was anything but an arena of conflict-free, creative play. My oedipal struggles were all tangled up with my competitive desires. They left me as inhibited and confused about my gender identity as I was later inhibited and confused about my sexual identity. With my Ben Hogan sabers in hand, I played a high stakes game of kill or be killed as judged by how many strokes I played over par for 18 holes relative to my competition. Every combatant was a stand-in for my father, or my older brother. This left me in a state of nearly dissolving panic. My neuromuscular coordination so betrayed me in these moments that had I understood what Parkinson's disease was, this too would have become an object of my neurotic worries. Whatever rhythm and timing I had developed in practice disappeared in competition. I was a basket case and did not know how to help myself.

Naomi demonstrated to me that you did not have to have a penis to be a phallic personality.

For her part, my aunt's unexamined "wishful" thought was that her chubby able-bodied and "people pleasing" nephew would run with the legs she did not have. Running became for me what arthritis was for my aunt over my entire lifetime: an unending opportunity for me to prove that I could fight the good fight. I went to college and soon started running.

If you pay close attention to a play or a movie, there will be subtle artistic devices that foreshadow storms to descend on the main characters. Naomi might have been "Superwoman" for many years, but even superheroes have their kryptonite and Naomi's Achilles heel was about to flare up. A perfect storm brewed as my Uncle Chuck's health deteriorated. His addiction to alcohol, the daily consumption of quarts of Rheingold beer soon determined a catastrophic vascular crisis. "Esophageal varices develop when normal blood flow to the liver is obstructed by scar tissue in the liver or a clot. Seeking a way around the blockages, blood flows into smaller blood vessels that are not designed to carry large volumes of blood. The vessels may leak blood or even rupture, causing life-threatening bleeding," writes the Mayo Clinic. This was my uncle. Soon he would bleed to death, a symptom of alcohol-induced liver disease.

Meanwhile back at the farm, having graduated to living in a cramped rectangular studio apartment on East End Avenue in Manhattan, I had fallen head over heels for a female runner I helped coach in my unofficial capacity as assistant woman's track coach for The Central Park Track Club. Lana was an irresistible catalyst for me to repeat history and attempt through merger to repair the damage done to my dreams of being a more socially and professionally competent human being. The inescapable fact was that Lana was irresistible on a host of levels. I was as stuck on her as a mouse on a glue trap. She was an amalgam of my family members' strengths and weaknesses, yet just different enough from them to tantalize me with the possibility that I could, through the passionate force of my character, mold her into the attachment figure I pined for. To be honest with myself now as I was rarely then, I longed for her to empower me to be the man I wished to be while holding my hand every step of the way. Yes, I know now this is an oxymoronic wish, and no, I could not see this foolhardiness back then. Hey, why let irreconcilable realities spoil a delicious fantasy?

What made for my magnetic attraction to Lana? Well, for starters she was enamored of the passionate dedication and intelligent curiosity I brought to my role as coach. I was a highly absorbent sponge or if you prefer, sucker for such attentions. Lana rigorously attended to those for whom she cared. By 1981, if there was one place I was most comfortable in my skin, it was on the track and on the roads. My resume as a runner was esteem building, if not spectacular by competitive standards. My personal records (PRs) were 2:55 in the marathon, 17:42 at 5000 meters (if my memory serves me correctly), and 29:56 for 5 miles. These statistics were not empirical grounds for the coaching hierarchy of my track club to install me as an assistant coach. While I focused on feverish attempts to impress these guys and hopefully hide my devalued self, they were much more interested in their assessment of my studious approach to the sport as a potential benefit to an overflow group of novice female runners. More often than not, my parents had ants in their pants and had "checked out" when as a child I yearned for them to appreciate the fruits of my meaning-making capacities. I mistook their hair-trigger, traumatized brains as a thumbs-down on the harvest of my playful imagination. That was a false attribution on my part. The only one blind to my intuitive gifts for learning and teaching was me seeing myself through the blank disconnected stares of my recollected parents. Those in the running community who knew and liked me paid attention to and had no problem graciously recognizing my gifts.

Once the women's head coach designated me as his assistant, I was immediately as good as gold to the eyes of my new students. If it crossed any of their minds to ask about my qualifications, they kept these questions to themselves. By disposition, I basked in the aura of my athletes' admiring gazes. I was the only one shocked as hell by my ability to demonstrate the creative flexibility and perceptive skills to serve a broad range of learning styles. I remained an impostor to myself through the recollected eyes of my parents.

When Lana happened on one of our workouts she witnessed me at my absolute best. She was as stellar a student of running as she was of medicine. This accomplished clinician, professor and researcher took an immediate liking to little old me. I was flattered beyond being flattered.

A cerebral, athletic, psychologically-minded, and good-natured feminist was in my book a femme fatale on the order of Sharon Stone's character in the film Basic Instinct. Lana's sex appeal for me was off the charts, and I am not sure if it mattered one bit what she looked like. The day she tenderly removed stitches from my head sustained during an automobile accident was the day I confused my ardor for her with visceral recollections of my early love affair with my mother. I was quick to confound my responses to Lana's ministrations as budding adult love. However, it was not, as the bud of my maturation was years from opening.

I cast Lana in the latest production of my ongoing family drama as "the great healer." My father was the great pretender to the throne of "medical expert" owing to his lay knowledge of antibiotics working as a wholesale pharmaceutical clerk. My brother had the "intellectual goods" and scientific acumen to survive medical school but, in my estimation, by the time he reached adolescence had grown weary of listening to our father try to foist the role of family "medicine doctor" onto him while being tone deaf to his own son's voice.

"The Body Keeps Score" is the pithy and eloquent title of Dr. Bessel van der Kolk's cutting edge investigation into the etiology and treatment of posttraumatic stress. The title is spot on in capturing the footprint of trauma on my family. Our bodies told the unthinkable and unspeakable stories of traumatic violations to our physical and emotional integrity. Our muscles and joints, as well as gastrointestinal, cardiovascular and immune systems, could not absorb the excess neural excitation we feared might blow our minds. We were perpetually mired in, or on the edge, of fights for survival with phantom demons, the origins of whose birth may have predated us by generations. These demons thrived on instinctual fear and the dominance of automatic, hard-wired neural circuits primed to ensure our survival. Our bodies kept score of what our minds could not put in perspective; that is, to discriminate real from imagined or recollected threats to our survival. All of our minds were "Benedict Arnolds" to us. They were the last places any of us looked for redemptive healing.

"Physician heal thyself" was a futile exhortation to rally troops that had dropped their arms, gone AWOL, scattered in all directions, removed their uniforms and disappeared amongst the local residents. Even though I was already in treatment for one year by the time I met Lana, I had about as much faith in rewiring and re-regulating a nervous system gone haywire as I would today in solving the puzzle that is a computer virus wreaking havoc with my operating software. I tend towards being more a technophobe than computer geek. My abiding belief was that my chronic infections and injuries were less mind over matter and more a matter of being minded by a competent doctor. Perhaps I hoped to kill two birds with one stone if Lana's love were to end my lonely and sickly existence.

Please pardon me overlooking a minor detail in the calculus of our ill-fated infatuation.

Lana was gay. I guess you might say that if love conquers all then why could it not bridge incompatible sexual identities. While in the throes of the temporary state of insanity that love can cause, Lana's sexual orientation was just a minor complication standing in the way of my imagined "happy ever after" ending to this relationship. Lana cohabitated with a very personable woman named Sharon, to my mind just another minor wrinkle to iron out before Lana was all mine. Even if I flattered myself to believe Sharon was my rival, she was still impossible to dislike.

Lana openly discussed with me thoughts of ending her domestic arrangement. I was like some long-time unemployed tradesman camped out on line, fervent with hope to qualify for the job of my dreams as Lana's boyfriend. This triangle was reminiscent of dynamics with my parents. It appeared that I was my mother's favorite, but in truth my father's needs took precedence over mine in what became a shifting zero sum game. Someone in my home always got attention at the expense of another in a manner that stimulated unending jealousy. I may have been my mother's emotional confidante, but I was nonetheless a child, and I could not, nor ever would have, displaced my father in the marital bed – as much as my mother sang my praises while feeding my father a steady diet of criticism.

Lana never raised my hopes that our friendship had anything to do with her plans to leave Sharon. It was Dr. G's prescient prediction that Lana would more likely leave Sharon for a Betsy or a Karen before a Mitchell, even had I been a "big boy," (my disparagement not his), as opposed to a little boy. Lana may have made out with me, and even consented to have sex one afternoon, in what might have been the most dissatisfying sexual encounter of her life. Yet if you put a gun to either of our heads, the answer to what end of the sexuality continuum she fell was a no brainer. The strength of my affections was not to inspire a change in her sexual orientation.

At the end of the day, my neediness for Lana to validate me as worthwhile and infuse my life with meaning became burdensome for her. Meanwhile, anxiety began to eat away at my love for coaching. I had no white-collar professional prospects at the time. To parlay this internship as coach into a paid profession required a graduate degree for most not in possession of resumés as star athletes. This daunting challenge had my parents' worried, impatient, and doubting voices fill the space between my ears. Would I quit again as I had law school? It was one thing to get through college funded by my parents. It was another matter to take myself seriously and borrow funds I did not have in my bank account. Lana was not in the market for a husband. So my uninspiring vocational future did not put her off. However, pining and whining in self-pity over seeing her so sparingly slowly and surely pushed her away.

As fate would have it, Lana sprained her ankle badly on the bridal path in Central Park one autumn day as the falling leaves created an illusion of a smooth and even surface that obscured some dangerous crevices left by horses who galloped daily along the path. As our Tuesday evening track workouts were our dates to rendezvous, and Lana could not participate for the foreseeable future, our time together shrunk to nothing.

Meanwhile, I fired a nearly fatal bullet into my relationship to Naomi, and this bullet, which exited the relationship, did extensive collateral damage to other family relationships in solidarity with Naomi. After Naomi's husband Chuck's funeral, I concocted some lie to excuse my absence from my Uncle's graveside service. In fact, I spent the afternoon with Lana. Yes, that was one of the poorest and most selfish judgments of a life littered with shameful low lights. I became so identified with my embarrassment and shame that I never told anyone, including Naomi, the truth about dishonoring myself, her and my uncle.

By this time in my life, every fiber of my being worked strenuously to discourage family members, whose needs I felt enslaved by, from expecting anything from me. Instead of thoughtless submission to them, I was now in my late 20's engaged in thoughtless rebellion against all the power they in reality no longer wielded over me. I was very much an emotional adolescent way beyond the years that such behaviors are acceptable in most family cultures. One day I sat with my Aunt Naomi in her apartment perhaps less than a year removed from the death of husband, Uncle Chuck. My dearth of appreciation for how my actions affected others left me in a state of shock as if rear ended by a car when Naomi turned on me. Her belligerent ambush thrust me into the shoes of General George Custer at Little Big Horn. Here was my aunt who had never asked much of me … asking me to give her money each month. Money for me at that stage was my emotional worry blanket. I woke up each morning expectant that I was one thoughtless misstep from homelessness. Granted, I bounced checks at times but this was due to lazy neglect of my checkbook ledger. I was not about to lose my then-job as a bellman. I paid my bills and finally had a little money left over to explore my artistic sensibilities. I certainly did not have funds to subsidize my aunt's household budget.

What threw me for a loop was that my Naomi had money and meanwhile she demanded money that I did not have. I do not believe Naomi had any knowledge or concern that I perceived her request as if she were an earlier edition of my overly needy and emotionally incestuous mother who overwhelmed me with demands that her little boy compensate beyond his capacities for deprivations she suffered at the hands of my often cruel father.

This episode sealed my deal on taking flight in the name of self-preservation from those who might re-traumatize me, on purpose or not. I had finally developed a strategy to combat my tendency to freeze when confronted by an attachment figure's disapproval. My strategy was to run. So run I did.

Unfortunately, I felt as if I took along with me and carried her burdens for many years. I did not realize why it was so hard for me to transfer the many lessons I had learned through running to other spheres of my life. The fact of the matter was that I identified so many of these lessons with my Aunt's strengths. I left her undeserving of using them for my personal joy and satisfaction. It never dawned on me that I carried with me the desire on both our parts to escape our losses. This broken symbiosis was too much for me to bear because I was still reeling from my broken symbiosis with my mother. By this juncture, Naomi, or anyone else for that matter, had the wrong guy to believe that I would sit passively by and permit them to subjugate me. My fledgling autonomous wings were mine, and I would take evasive actions to not lose them.

I also think that on some level Naomi pushed me away because she did not want me to see her this way. I believe my aunt wanted to hide her humiliating vulnerabilities in the throes of grief. Her worst fear was to be a burden to anyone, and I was already a burden to myself. She defensively beat me to the punch.

In part to fill the vacuum left by my disappearance, my resourceful aunt gathered herself, hired members of her building superintendent's family to assist her around the house, and continued to receive the loyal support of my brother, sister-in-law, and to a lesser degree, my parents. Sadly, with my uncle out of the picture, Naomi pretty much lived under the equivalent of house arrest.

By 1989, after seven years of intensive psychoanalytic psychotherapy, I could hear Carole King's refrain "It's too late baby now it's too late" and not become a puddle of tears. In tribute to the collaboration between myself and Dr. G who helped me hatch, build, and reprogram this self of mine, I was now prepared to take on marriage and apply to graduate school in social work. Naomi, the Aunt, who adored me for the first 28 years of my life, from that point forward fashioned me as a stingy, self-absorbed, ingrate of a nephew, a deserving object of her spite and vindictiveness to the bitter end. I will grant her assessments of stingy and self-absorbed without argument. However, I do not now accept that I deserved her spiteful vindictiveness (though I did believe so for too many years). Locked in some dissociated vault was her love for me.

By 1989, Naomi's health had further deteriorated and she made it known to me through the executor of her estate – my brother – that my modest inheritance was to be withheld if I skipped out on her graveside service as I had skipped out on the burial of her husband. Not many months from entering hospice care, Naomi was inclined to do everything in her power to defend against the shame and humiliation of being stood up at her own funeral. Little did Naomi know that she had absolutely nothing to worry about.

I was building a life worth preserving and had assembled a diverse enough and large enough pit crew to help regulate the emotional flooding that had previously resulted in my flight.

In fact, I very much wanted Sue, my fiancée, to meet Naomi before she passed. Sue knew a little about the rift between us, and she knew a great deal more about how much Naomi had meant to me growing up.

God bless her: Despite being wracked by pain and fatigue, when Sue and I visited, Naomi gathered her rumpled bed sheets and hospital-issued nightgown and tried her best to be presentable for company. I will forever be indebted to her for letting bygones be bygones, even if it was just for 30 minutes. Naomi was at her self-deprecating, lighthearted best that day. For Sue and I, in our thirties and beginning a life together, endings were not on our minds. Yet, here we were with a dying woman who could not have been more comfortable with her imminent fate. My aunt was polite, in-quisitive, and delighted by the visit. On the way out I kissed my Aunt for the very last time (and for the first time in many years), and then whispered in her ear that I loved her.

Naomi had brokered a deal with my sister-in-law, Lisa, that when she could no longer raise one finger she would surrender to the biological laws that all living things eventually return to a state of quiescence. She was good to her word as always. When Naomi could not muster the strength to raise one finger, she dispatched my sister-in-law and the hospice worker from her apartment and died as she lived, on her terms.

I would like to think Naomi would have been proud of me on the day of her burial. Not only did I show up, but I delivered her eulogy and took my medicine like a man. It was my mea culpa in front of the family tribunal for having distanced myself from my aunt's vilification the last years of her life. I stood tall, honored my aunt for her many admirable qualities, and hoped my family would cease to shoot daggers in my direction for distancing myself from them as an act of preserving the seeds of my autonomous life from being babied to death. I did not foresee that they would cease to beat me up long before I gave myself a break. The setting was sur-real. It felt like a demonstration of my family's moral superiority, as if they were saying, "We are big enough people to forgive you once you eat crow in our presence."

I believe today that had Aunt Naomi lived into her ninth de-cade and discovered a modicum of patience with the slowness of my own maturation process, she would have looked over at me from across her kitchen table while eating her canned tuna and Ritz crackers and found a spitting image of her strength, disci-pline, passion, determination, and courage all wrapped up in the service of living a dignified life. I love you Aunt Naomi for all your shortcomings even if I am yet only learning to tolerate mine. I feel very fortunate that my shrinks have taught me how to pack them up, take them on the road with me and refuse to turn back, no matter what, until I reach my destination. I know, dearest Aunt, that had you grown up in a different time and had circumstances been different for you, the road I travel these days is the road you would have cleared and paved for me.

CHAPTER 5

SUPER SLOW MOTION REPLAYS OF RERUNS THAT BECAME FIRST RUNS

S low motion replay, a 1960s' innovation, permitted football fans to examine the intricacies of the fast-paced chess game of football. Famed New York sportscaster Warner Wolff invited his audience to put their coaching hats on with his signature call: "Let's go to the videotape." What looked in real time like a running back weaving his way through a chaotic bombardment of human projectiles, now in slow motion assumed the look of an intuitive, part-choreographed and part-improvised dance. With instant replay, for the first time fans marveled at a taste of the supercomputing capacities of world-class athletes "in states of flow," the experience of what they refer to as "slowing the game down," splitting fractions of seconds into fractions.

I have never sat with an NFL quarterback or coach as they deconstructed film of their last game, although I have pursued a similar collaborative process on both sides of the couch as patient and treatment provider. The impact of mutual influence over time can reengineer someone's lens, which in turn yields new perspectives on the complexities of history revisited. Sometimes my lens was better equipped than others to process memories as wide-angle pictures in motion. Other times my lens was hijacked by automatic survival mechanisms, and I saw life through the eyes of those who rigidly and reflexively made a dynamic world fit into their old static narratives.

I like slow-motion replay as a metaphor to understand the process by which we rewrite our narratives and open new possibilities to free up and channel creative energy to adapt to changing circumstances. Psychoanalysts join with patients to replay memories in slow motion. We use our critical thinking to challenge and scrutinize assumptions. We discover over time, surprisingly if not shockingly, that we have clung to patently false and unprocessed assumptions as if they were guideposts for effective living arrived at through extensive empirical research.

We all are required to trust our imperfect critical faculties to keep us safe, or else we may be at perpetual risk of making over learned scripts that are hazardous to our health and welfare into self-fulfilling prophecies. Super slow motion replay has become a staple for sports officials adjudicating athletic contests. In this chapter, super slow-motion replay is a way to conceptualize emotional intelligence in action, when our minds operate on all integrated and coordinated cylinders. Time slows down, information processing speeds up, and we see in high definition the nuances of relationships with a wider-angle lens. Often in defensive postures we are emotionally blind to or selectively ignore important sectors of our fields of vision that produce anxious conflicts. Psychotherapy patients, whether or not they understand the process in these terms, learn in treatment to engineer or reengineer these faculties of mind. An effective treatment alliance opens up space between the frames of virtual film to expand the thematic and dynamic potential of stories yet to be written. Therapist and patient hopefully disprove as false and mourn as futile the patient's "relentless hope" (thanks to Dr. Martha Stark for this nugget of a term), to change history. They free up and channel energies for creative mastery formerly stuck between their wishes to change history and their fears of failure to do so.

When we slow down unfolding recollections and insert an observing and reflective lens between the frames, we create space to develop new perspectives and choices. We relate to the next moment changed by the current moment and armed with a never ending, evolving set of paradigms.

We learn that each moment is a yet unborn experience to be co-constructed in an infinite number of ways by networks of information and energy exchanges whose intricacies and breadth are ineffable.

An old psychoanalytic supervisor of mine, Dr. B, likened the eyes of such a projector to those owned by someone who is part pilgrim and part scientist. To revise the stories of our lives we develop a curious, kind, compassionate, open-minded, and accepting lens we trust ourselves to use responsibly. To confidently and seamlessly shift among the roles of director, cinematographer, and camera man is to demystify, unseat, and re-edit the images interpreted by those less equipped than ourselves yet nonetheless, in many cases long after their deaths, still blindly telling our stories for us.

I share with you now my best recollection of an event long ago interred into my unconscious and now exhumed to breathe new life into this rotting legacy. Behold how my reexamination of this "forensic" evidence offered me a wellspring of great hope and optimism for the future.

The pink Spalding rubber ball leaked through my hands as if it were liquid as it trickled out into the street. I was 11 years old, living in the Flatbush section of Brooklyn, a suburban ghetto of attached two-family houses. This was home to an exploding class of first- and second-generation middle-class nouveau riche. These families who gave birth to the Baby Boomer generation inhabited an era of newfound prosperity. Our Jewish namesakes were spirits of so many who were psychologically crushed and incinerated during the sequential apocalyptic periods of the Great Depression and World War II.

We prepubescent Boomers behaved as if the de facto Parks, Recreation and Cultural Affairs Administration for Brooklyn. In our endless munificence, we declared our block a permanent street fair. Here whiffle ball, punch ball, touch football, and roller hockey were the norm, only occasionally interrupted by trespassing motorists. Those drivers who lived in this community of Mill Basin, built atop a reclaimed landfill, knew better than to cruise any faster than 10 to 15 mph on this makeshift asphalt playground.

I remember one summer evening in 1965: Dusk had softened the spotlight on our play while I daydreamed of heroic triumphs. My mind was in Shea Stadium about 19 ½ miles away as the crow flies. This evening I imagined myself performing a more polished version of the Keystone Cop-like feats of my idols the New York Mets. The sound of automobile engines bled into the chirrups of cicadas.

What happened next was anything but slow motion. Maybe because my mind was elsewhere or maybe because I was not the most talented baseball player on the block, I flubbed a catch ... and without thinking, ran out into the street in pursuit of my errant drop. In a fraction of a second, from out of my left eye I caught an oncoming car bearing down on me. I heard brakes screech and saw the car lurch to a stop, only inches from my left hip. I froze with instinctual fear. Like the incandescence of a dying firefly, I might have been here one second and then gone for good. My first coherent thought after finding I still had a pulse was my existential dread of facing my Dad.

Based on history, I felt certain my father was about to publicly shame me for not keeping myself out of harm's way. There was no way for me to flee this active crime scene and not get fingered. Too many eyes were trained on me to quickly dig a hole and disappear underground or deny that I was the culprit who disturbed the relaxed atmosphere of the block. Would habitual tendencies dictate the day? Was Dad about to give me hell for disrupting his post-dinner rituals?

What happened next was nearly more of a shock to the system than being run over by a menacing motorist. Dad had aggravated an old back injury first sustained jumping into a foxhole during World War II many times over. For the rest of his life, which ended in 2004, he complained about his bad back with the same predictability and regularity of a noon church bell. Typically, my father invoked his disability to beg off having to play with me. Little did I realize back then that by asking him to play catch with me, I drew attention to his guilt and shame over opting out of parental duties. Sadly he wanted no part of this responsibility and therefore never realized that he could choose to accept his failing or change his ways. Dad used his disability to "act out" wishes to reclaim the prerogatives of childhood "to be," and "not have to do," taken prematurely from him by the exigency that was his family's fight to scrape pennies together during the Great Depression.

Out of mercy for both of us, such requests became little more than a trickle from a water faucet turned off by age six or seven. I had learned the hard way by that time to not draw attention to behaviors unbecoming to a dignified father. When I did, he projected onto me his dearth of empathetic concern for my wish to bond with him and then damned me for my unloving nature.

Now to my utter shock and amazement here came Dad lumbering down the street in his best middle-aged impression of a sprint. On a ladder of miracles, this was only a rung below that of my Aunt Naomi lifting her paralyzed lower half out of her wheelchair to run to my rescue. How did my father manage to run down the block, herniated discs, depression, PTSD, and all? Well, my current rudimentary adult understanding of the human endocrine system in crisis suggests that Dad's paternal instinct to protect his legacy kicked in and his internal pharmacy dispensed adrenaline and endorphins sufficient for him to temporarily "feel no pain."

This did not compute for me in 1965. Even more surprising is what happened when he reached me. My father spoke softly and inquisitively, as if he was a trainer checking with thoughtful concern for his possibly injured athlete. I told Dad I was fine and a look of relief washed over his face. Convinced I was no worse for wear, he reversed his tracks and walked back to our apartment with his signature duck-like waddle.

Both of us seemed to put this regrettable episode behind us as quickly as possible. Dad never mentioned it again, and since I felt lucky enough to have dodged two bullets that evening, I was all for this decree of silence. And yet when I sifted through such memories on a psychoanalytic couch, this is one I returned to many times over in search of all it had to offer to synthesize new perspectives for a narrative of self-renewal.

Memories are part fact and part constructed fiction. They are copies of experiences passed on as historical records, suffused with wishes, fantasies, and defenses that distort for better and for worse what took place. Objectivity is a theoretical and unattainable ideal. The more these recollections are re-transcribed over time, the more they become as falsified as what happens to the messages re-transcribed during a game of "telephone." So I am aware that rolling the videotape of this recollection, or any other, is a little bit like being an artist, archaeologist and anthropologist seeking to piece together the fractured artifacts of a history.

My father's out of character display of compassion for this 11-year-old must have held the potential to violently tear at the weave of an image of my father that begged me to keep a safe distance from him. Did I dare even consider dropping my armor just as Reagan had considered destroying our nuclear arsenals after the 1966 meeting with Soviet President Gorbachev that eased

Cold War tensions between the two superpowers? Such a question had to be too discombobulating for an 11-year-old left to his own devices to assess his personal risks. It makes abundant sense to me that the specter of such agonizing conflict was cause for me to immediately repress this freshly-minted memory. At risk here was an experience so incongruent with what I had relied upon to keep myself safe (several arms lengths away from my father) that it held the potential to throw me into "crazy-making" anxious conflict. Who was this man, and could I be trusted to know him or anyone if left to my own devices to fend for myself in the urban jungle?

Such questions begged to be asked, revisited, examined, and worked through many times over as an adult in treatment. Had I more command of myself at this age I would not have repressed and thus passed on asking the following questions: "How come you weren't mad at me?" or "How come you were able to run to see if I was okay but couldn't run after or bend over to pick up a ball?" I knew intuitively, had I asked such questions, Dad was certain to dismiss me to avoid his own internal discord.

My life as a child was littered with attachment figures who could not distinguish personal responsibility from damning blame. My father was not capable of containing and learning from the dissonance between his laudable behavior this evening and the less laudable behavior on his parenting resume. So I unconsciously and automatically expunged the memory from my historical narrative, to my short-term safety and long-term detriment.

Another interesting retrospective question, overlooked at the time, is whether or not my unsupervised state was or was not a parental indiscretion. Were they both habitually asleep at the wheel, and if so, was I an accident waiting to happen such as the one that took place on this prophetic evening. How did I dare imagine taking charge of a self, rife with confusion and self-doubt, only to see how clearly my parents were mindless in their collective operation of the ship I lived on? My motto was better to walk through life ignorant of one's defective identity than to risk panic over the recognition of a self of little or no useful management value.

I cannot count for you the number of times as an adult running through the streets of Manhattan, I carelessly came very close to adding my name to the number of traffic fatalities. Might we conjecture that this reckless behavioral pattern was shaped by the meaning-making apparatus of an immature mind who concluded: "If Dad was not worried about my impulsiveness nearly getting me killed, then did I decide that I had nothing to worry about, or was not worth caring about?"

Clearly this pattern went unmodified for many years, as I continued to throw my gambler's dice. The notion of caring for myself was a process that evolved and revolved around learning to trust my imperfect yet dependable meaning-making capacities. The 11-year-old version of me learned that questioning his parents' performance damned him as an ungrateful and disrespectful child. So it took having a shrink by my side for moral support before I gave myself permission as an adult to see the error of their ways without reflexively covering my head as if expecting a verbal slap. My dependent 11-year-old mind could not accept the reality that Dad was selfishly disconnected and indifferent to my needs.

No, my politically correct take on such benign neglect would have been that I was "making a mess of my play time and shame on me for not doing a better job of fending for myself." My not-so-misbegotten expectation that evening was for Dad to publicly humiliate me and tattoo the words "shameful burden" on my forehead. I heard my father silently screaming behind his yelling: "Hadn't I considered what the neighbors might think about him if his 11-year-old son did not know enough to look both ways before running out into the street?" No, I had not. Often, in anticipation of such responses, I would beat him to the punch, hopeful that my acts of contrition might preempt his sadistic investment in lashing me with his serpentine tongue.

Were there other ways to understand my father's shocking re-action? Who was this tender impostor? To take this side of him in was to potentially throw my mind into a nonsensical state of chaos the way cyber terrorists throw into disarray the operating systems of corporate and government computers. Dad's hypocritical and illogical messages had already confused me to the point of dis-trusting myself completely and wishing desperately to buy into his conceits. Was the miracle possible for me to find comfort in this oxymoronic moment? Could the life-altering screech of a driver trying desperately to stop his momentum have awoken my father from sleep walking through a life scripted early on?

The adhesive that over time would help hold my self-concept together was my growing tolerance of human beings as studies in contradictions. Dad was in truth cruel, sadistic, tactless ... and in fairness also affectionate, devoted, and an adequate provider of ba-sic needs. The dissonance of his behavior earlier on was like a solvent that threatened to destroy the adhesives holding myself together.

I had learned early on to be the archivist for misery-perpetuating story lines. The story I told myself was that I did not care enough about my father to control my impulse to chase the ball into the street and was thus undeserving of his tender loving care. By incor-rectly confusing his mind with mine, I was convinced he thought that if I had cared more for him, such carelessness would not have happened and I would have not forced him to get off his duff and risk further displacement of his vertebral discs.

This story line preserved and energized my "relentlessly defen-sive and intractable hope" that the day I made my father proud, and thus cured him of his self-perpetuated unhappiness, I would then earn my just desserts to make my ascent up Abraham Maslov's hierarchy of needs (https://www.simplypsychology.org/maslow. html) to become worthy of more than the parental provision of basic needs in times of sickness, injury, or emergency.

As I saw it through my youthful conflict-avoidant lens, Dad came running because I was important enough to be kept alive as the repository for his shattered hopes and dreams, to be actualized when I was old enough to fulfill said dreams with my hypothetical dazzling accomplishments.

My patients often ask me if what they are saying makes sense. Often, without realizing it, they are asking for the first time whether some viewpoint forced on them, which they learned to dare not think about or question makes logical sense. The other question often linked to this one is: Can I count on your empathy, compassion, acceptance, and support if I dare betray these internal images of my caregivers? Even more importantly perhaps, a patient may need to know that I will not become the incarnation of his worst fears of that person, even if provoked.

With the benefit of psychoanalysis and training I have often replayed this memory. I have come to frame Dad's actions as a hard-wired, unconsciously determined and executed survival mechanism that jolted him free for the duration of this short-lived crisis from over-learned prescribed patterns of behavior. These habits were sets of internal dictates that "took care of him" in ways he implicitly believed he could not do for himself. In the twilight of a near historic moment, my father adaptively mobilized his resources to fend off a potential family tragedy of horrific proportions, one that would have irreparably ripped at and further damaged his already tattered identity. When the crisis passed, my father, drained by the spectre of the near loss of my life or limbs, wanted nothing more than to be swaddled by relief.

Dad's tragic flaw was that he lacked an observing and reflective lens capable of reprocessing old narratives to open up new possibilities for being him. Thus, he was unwilling and unable to suspend disbelief that another human being, who was not nor could ever be the parent he wished for, might still help him expand his choice points. He never sought treatment.

In truth, my father was neither the problem nor the solution to my dilemmas in life once the die was cast on my internal object world. Likewise, I too was neither the cause of his misery nor the solution. Though my father may have been more limited than myself by dint of family and cultural traumas, both of us were also more resilient and adaptive in our own individual ways than anyone gave us credit for. The seeds of my healthy growth and development were planted by extended family members, friends' parents, and a series of empowering teachers.

My father's younger brother bailed our family out of a financial crisis when blood poisoning abruptly ended Dad's career as a printer. My Uncle Bernie ensured my family a lower middle-class lifestyle until my father's retirement. Dad managed to work, raise a family, and avoid self-medicating himself with alcohol and drugs despite suffering symptoms of post-traumatic stress disorder his entire adult life.

By clinging to the fraudulent notion that my father was much more of a malingerer than he truly was, I incubated the false belief that I was to blame for his inability to transcend his pains. My brother also certified this idea, probably in part to feel less guilty about hating a father who neglected him and dumped the hat of surrogate father (to me) on his head. In truth, Dad did the best he could without psychiatric care, and it took years for me to separate myself from him enough to realize that my brother and I were not alone in living adult lives filled with injustice.

This realization broadened into the recognition that my expectation – that adult peers would reject me as wanting – was nothing but an artifact of history. There was no truth to the supposition that I was not smart enough, strong enough, or successful enough to garner his praise. Dad's issues cast a dark and foreboding pall over his life, and almost nothing made him happy except to reminisce with his buddies about the days before he went off to war, a life changed forever by a cataclysm that threatened to end for everyone the free pursuit of happiness.

CHAPTER 6

IT'S NEVER TOO LATE TO REWRITE TRAGEDIES INTO TRIUMPHS OF THE HUMAN SPIRIT

By 1982, after years of being sidelined with overuse injuries and strange viral-like symptoms of an immune system compromised by excessive physical and emotional stress, I was once again healthy and training. Fortunately, my addictive appetite to run increasingly faster times was a thing of the past. I constitutionally lacked the natural foot speed and the stout physical constitution to endure the shock waves to my spine and connective tissues produced by the constant pounding on asphalt. Having climbed out of the hellhole of addiction, once the promised Nirvana, I lost all incentive to put my body through trials it was never suited for.

My unhealthy, formerly glorified, relationship to running became one of relative disinterest. No longer did I believe that my motivation and competence to perform rudimentary activities of daily living hinged on some recommended daily dose of running as if a cocktail of Prozac, vitamins, and Red Bull. A satisfying shift took place as I reclassified running to extremes, as a problem of daily living and not a solution. The loneliness of the long distance runner lost its romantic allure.

This led me to intensive psychotherapy with Dr. G. Dr. G was the antithesis of my father, a walking billboard for the virtues of taking one's self seriously. This English-born, Cambridge graduate and former amateur boxer traveled to the U.S. courtesy of a Fulbright scholarship and earned a Ph.D. in comparative literature from the University of Michigan. In 1973 he switched his profession to psychology and earned a certificate in psychodrama from a small institute in NYC. Later, in 1990, he would earn a second Ph.D. in counseling psychology from New York University. What a slug! Short of him loving me the way I wished my father had loved me, I hated the bastard as an ambitious standard bearer who left me painfully self-conscious of a truth I wanted no ownership of – that my life's resumé (by comparison) was woefully short of professional accomplishments. When we started working together in 1981, I was 27 and he was 40, a distinguished-looking bearded and prematurely gray psychotherapist who could have passed as much older than his age.

Dr. G. took himself and our work very seriously. He loved me in an analytic sense by recognizing the good, bad, and the ugly sides of me and deeming me as worthwhile and workable as an integrated whole. In spite of my childish demands to be treated like an entitled little prince, he did not waver in expecting more of me. For the first time in my life, when I got lost in some dissociated compartment of my mind, I had someone I trusted to tactfully tell me to "stop and look at where you are stepping."

I had permitted running to take over my life to fill the void that was defined by the absence of meaningful attachments to others and myself. Now my work with Dr. G. helped to fill the void left in the wake of my attempts to fulfill delusions of running grandeur. He became my de facto trainer for the mental muscles that had atrophied severely while in the throes of my activity addiction – the atrophying of emotional skills like frustration tolerance, impulse control, patience, regulation, reasoning, judgment, and resilience that collectively rendered me unfit to complete attempts at graduate programs. Life Chiropractic College had gone the same direction as my introductory classes in sports psychology at Columbia University. When the going got tough, I could not muster the wherewithal to tough it out.

Dr. G's radical vision for me as a center of initiative possessed of my own propulsion engine encouraged me to rethink my inner map cobbled together by recollections of how my parents saw and treated me. I prayed that my faith in Dr. G and this arcane process of personal transformation would permit me to rework an identity shaped by my parents' needs. Still, I lived with a nagging foreboding that even with Dr. G present to help me contain my anxieties, I might still come apart at the seams should I compel the parents I had internalized to release their grip on me. Without these images holding together my self-concept, would I become some hastily glued together and rained on school project made of construction paper? Any identity, even one that I reviled, served the purpose of assigning value. I feared that without this identity I would be regarded, and by extension, regard myself, as the remains of some organic material charred beyond recognition; useless and worthless.

I do not recall how many years it took me to begin taking longer and longer furloughs from my neurotic prison. Maybe it was the same amount of time it took Andy Dufresne, protagonist of the 1994 movie "Shawshank Redemption," to burrow his escape from prison. How long did it take Andy? Was it 17 years? The pivotal concept was that, unlike my parents, or my brother for that matter, I trusted Dr. G to support me while I slowly took the reins of my own life back from outdated unconscious habits of being.

The linchpin for this shift was a mindful dismantling of the belief that my early life condemned me to a stagnant existence. I might still on occasion feel deprived, victimized, left out, and inadequate, but like some hoarder who had gone into treatment and developed an autonomous perspective on an inventory of junk cluttering his personal space, I now achieved a fresh perspective on these archetypes. What I once held as priceless truths were now exposed as largely worthless. One day I hoped to awaken to a new reality in which these fictions could be discarded with the biodegradable garbage.

The germination of these seeds of hope began with experiments in artistic expression. Still, the specter of history made cultivating these seeds a formidable challenge. Growing up, my brother had taken lessons on the violin and accordion. My Dad saw this as money squandered. Would it really have made a difference to my father's happiness had Peter continued playing beyond a few short years? Would it have mattered if Peter had serenaded Dad atop the former World Trade Towers at his 65th birthday dinner? Somehow, I doubt anything would have cut the mustard.

For my part, I did not have the courage to ask to play an instrument. My father's dealings with my brother shaped my belief that unless I kissed his feet every day for the gift of an instrument or guaranteed that this investment would confer bragging rights to him in the neighborhood, then outlays for music lessons would never be a line item on his household budget. So you will not be shocked to hear that even if my father had offered music lessons, my rehearsed response would have been "thanks but no thanks." I preferred to never learn to play an instrument than to be beholden in that way.

I did nonetheless ask my parents to pay for a wooden recorder, which was a mandatory component of my primary education. I braced myself for the reaction of a father who had been mortified that his investment in my brother's lessons had not led to my brother becoming a virtuoso accordion player like Art Van Damne or violinist like Jascha Heifetz. I could not guarantee a virtuoso performance of "Row, Row, Row Your Boat" let alone anything that a person in their right mind would listen to voluntarily. So, to spare my father a second broken heart, I never asked for instruction.

But the desire for music never left me. In high school and college, as much as I yearned to be cast in theatrical productions and tour with singing groups, I remained on the sidelines. Steeped in rounds of rejection, bullying, and public humiliation, I was your human equivalent of a rescue dog. Repetitive trauma shaped anxious vulnerabilities that conditioned me to retreat from people and take refuge in cell-like, secure and isolated spaces. I was not above locking myself in off-the-beaten-path offices or bathrooms to enjoy relaxed solitude. Again, this desire for isolation was shaped by my parents, for whom boundaries were a foreign concept. These odd folks thought it cute to open the bathroom door and proudly take a picture of me on the toilet, pants hanging by my ankles. This image exemplified one in a very long series of humiliating and embarrassing invasions of privacy. You would not know it by the dampened look of mild surprise registered by the camera that I was completely mortified by their callous insensitivity to this humiliating public exposure. Well, the reason no one knew it was because not until decades later did Dr. G observe and name these feelings into existence.

Now, in 1982, the time finally arrived after years of hermit-like seclusion for loneliness to outweigh my lust to escape from such boundary violations. Even though I had to regularly fight my rationalizations for not actively participating in life, I was able to borrow Dr. G's trusted ego and reach for what I had missed: I went back to school to experiment with my gifts and interests in the performing arts.

Throwing myself wholeheartedly into artistic expression also helped me sublimate my longings for female companionship. My dating life remained as arid as a desert until I hit 30. Instead, I earned plenty of affection for investing creative energies in my classes. There is never a shortage of support for passionate students earnestly trying to apply the lessons offered by their instructors. If there was a class of people with whom I had been popular with from kindergarten on, it was teachers. That was even the case in ballet class, where after years of running and not stretching, the range of motion in my hips was almost as limited as my aunt's. I moved one direction very well, forward, and that was it. When my kids were younger, they mocked my gyrations on the dance floor as if I were a carbon copy of someone dancing in the grips of a hallucinogenic drug or inhabited by some spirit force during a religious revival. Perhaps, my sense of rhythm and grace was not what they hoped it to be. Either way, it did not take very long for me to realize that I did not have the grace or athleticism to dance on the stage of a community theater, let alone a professional stage. Still, the warm attentions of my instructors and helpful students energized me, and with their investment, the depression I had tried to combat for years with running was finally lifting.

Manhattan is a place you can rub elbows with the elite if you choose the right performance studios. I took tap dancing with Bob Audy and found myself tapping away next to Mandy Patinkin preparing for his starring role in the Broadway musical *Sunday in the Park with George*. My vocal coach had formerly trained Audrey Hepburn, and my songwriting coach was a Grammy nominee who had a number one hit on Billboard's top 100 to his credit. Even if I did not share the extraordinary talent of some of my fellow students, what I did share was the fire in my belly to create meaningful performances in my life.

Talent aside, what separated me from the "movers and shakers" was that while teachers and students sparked the flames of my imagination, between these sessions my pilot light went out, snuffed by low self-confidence and low self-esteem borne of extreme narcissistic vulnerabilities to the anticipated criticisms and rejections. Trying to re-light my imagination was like trying to strike a flame with wet matches that snapped interminably in my fingers. If I could not do something in short order, I became frustrated and figured it would never happen. As much as I was changing, the paradox of my existence was that I was still in many respects the same.

I was still unfortunately a bit of a prima donna and a potential legend in my own mind, able to deceive myself into believing that I could elevate myself to greatness without breaking a sweat. However, a grounded personal assessment was that I had more talent as a songwriter than the rest of the disciplines combined. This period marked the genesis of a heartfelt understanding that genuine passion, not to be confused with addictive cravings and terrors of attachment loss, was my engine for achievement.

For the next six years I wrote songs weekly, spent time in studios recording music demos, and visited my fair share of music publishers. My principal collaborator, Joe, was a songwriter destined for recording success. Joe believed in me as a lyricist more than I believed in myself, and the tension between these perspectives left me perpetually at odds with myself over who I really was. He took himself and his craft seriously and eventually saw in me a guy who talked a good game and played an uninspired one. Poor self-pitying me could not put myself in Joe's shoes and understand that it was in his best interests to give me a pink slip.

Meanwhile, I did my best impression of my mother reprising her favorite role, "The Passive-Aggressive Martyr." Joe discovered what most in my cramped universe discovered sooner or later: I left very little room for others' subjectivities that shed light on ugly parts of my nature. People got close to me at their own risk. My modus operandi was to portray myself as an innocent victim being attacked by whoever tried in vain to communicate my mistreatment of them. If the mirror being held up to me was unflattering, then the mirror as far as I was concerned was legally blind. When push came to shove, my intolerance of discomfiting conflict and ambivalence led me to push Joe away.

Unfortunately, my chronic allergies to unknowns and uncertainties molded the responses of music publishers to my original compositions as well. In fact, I rigidly erred on the side of cautiously covering my ass and not letting these publishers make their own independent evaluations of my artistic creations. No, I aggressively took the reins of my own rejection and never gave them a chance to thrust a Simon Cowell, *American Idol* dagger into the heart of my hopes for a platinum record. After prying open industry doors, I induced these music moguls to slam them in my face by failing to follow up with their requests to write a hit song for some artist in search of material. To be the architect of my own rejection was the lesser of two evils. I did not dare put my best foot forward and made certain to burn every bridge every chance I had before they were burned for me.

I met Joe in a workshop led by "Jim." In his heyday, Jim had been a top-shelf songwriter. As the corporatized music industry pushed songwriters to the sidelines, he morphed into a very able instructor in the art of songwriting. Jim was an equally good purveyor of empty dreams who saw in me a real rube receptive to his powers of suggestion. I flitted around his narcissistic aura like a moth orbiting a flame for the next six years. To this day, I am not sure my lyrical skills, absent the appeal of my runner's behind, boyish looks, and maternal sensibilities, merited an invitation to join his professional workshop.

If you can imagine for a moment a quality test to determine the limits of stress that load carrying components of an automobile engine can tolerate, then you understand that life in proximity to my mother was the libidinal equivalent of being jacked on amphetamines. My erogenous zones at every stage of development were over stimulated. You may or may not, depending on your own formative experiences, understand that having my genitals bathed by my mother until approximately age 10 left me with a brain wired to sexualize a whole host of nonsexual needs. Worse yet, not only did my father openly let me know he wanted me to be a girl, but he was one to not feel appropriately respected and loved if you did not honor him with Geisha-like deference. More closely identified with my mother than my father for a million reasons under the sun, I wondered for decades on end if I could win the admiration and praise of powerful men without prostituting myself, if not literally then figuratively. This was the million-dollar question I hoped to answer with Jim.

Let us just say that over the six years that spanned our acquaintance, I do not recall Jim once in the company of a girlfriend. A young man my age I will call "Fred," who was unemployed and subsidized by Jim, was reputed to be his biological son. Let's just say that I stuck myself between wanting Jim's fatherly admiration and praise for my lyrical creations and my fears that I would lose hope forever to be loved and respected by "real" men like my father if I did what I rigidly denied I needed to do, to run for the hills and never look back.

Had I been farther along the curve in the development of my emotional maturity, I would have recognized the potential for me to fall prey to his lustful designs on me.

My unconscious was primed to feed on the good of this relationship and not be infected by the bad. This in truth was the equivalent of trying to be half pregnant or alternately, to wish to remain in an abusive relationship and be spared the decimation of my self-esteem. I reluctantly admit to you that I paid for classes and accepted as fitting tribute to a man who welcomed me into his inner circle to clean his bathroom when conditions warranted it. I do not believe the school registrar was aware of the non-pecuniary tuition payments I made under the table or, should I say, under the toilet. You cannot make this stuff up. To end the suspense, he did not get beyond trying to grab my ass during a "friendly" embrace inside in his apartment. Still, it took some time for me to flee his lair. Jim had a knack for drawing you in and making you believe that you were privileged to ride his coattails to the recording success that was right around the corner if you played by his rules. I insinuated myself into his life and moved perilously close to making Jim the center of my universe.

He was, to this young man, still haunted by early abandonment traumas, an instigator of my worst insecurities. He would play the part of doting uncle, then inexplicably disconnect without explanation for four to seven days at a time, my multiple calls unanswered. When Jim resurfaced, he expressed malignant indifference and disdain for my fearful despair and dread that I had pissed him off to the point of cutting me off for good. Such attachment ruptures were for me the worst recapitulations of my mother who nurtured an unhealthy dependency on the illusion that she existed to meet my needs on demand, and then, when she needed a break, disconnected from my demanding nature, throwing me into a temporary state of panic.

My own reparative myth was that I had become a burden to Jim and needed to be subjected to a weaning off process for our mutual welfare. Sounds like the lament of a battered spouse, does it not? Years later I realized his crazy-making denials were designed to create sufficient doubt in my mind to dismiss apprehensions about his narcissism. Jim's unwillingness to dignify my muted rage and anger left me filled with shame and guilt. This was a cold adult edition of a child's game of "tag, you're it."

Between 1982 and 1988, I ran in place going nowhere fast in the thrall of this man. You will not be surprised to hear that, despite swearing up and down that his phoenix was right around the corner, this wildly talented man never managed to rise from the ashes. Heck, his resurgence was not right around the corner of Jupiter. Those who continued to ride his coattails did not exactly wind up with songs on Billboard's top 100.

I have never once doubted that Jim indeed taught me invaluable lessons in the art of songwriting. However, he taught me a more important lesson – everything that glitters is not gold and people with holes in their conscience will take the naïve hostage. I have come to believe that forgiveness is the only route to escaping the self-styled prison that kept me locked up in the past. And I see that in the early 1980s, Jim was just being Jim. It was up to me to take what he could offer in class and politely refuse his invitation to join a toxic extended family system outside of class. There are some whose lifetime accomplishments are healthier to admire from afar. He is one of those people.

I write this having been able to eventually pull myself free of his orbit. Much of the credit for this goes to Dr. G. When I first met Dr. G, I was living in a studio apartment, working a non-skilled sales job without a future and could not have bought a date. (Well, l in truth I could have but was too cheap to do so.) I had literally run myself into a gimpy-legged depression. By the time I moved on from his practice I was married, owned a home, had earned a Master's degree in social work and was one year short of being a first-time father.

Some credit for my transformation in this period and escape from what was at the time the dead-end songwriting also goes to Sue, who would become my first wife. She moved in "yuppified" circles that did not take kindly to her romance with a hack songwriter. Eventually, she issued the ultimatum that I could continue to ride Jim's train to nowhere or I could marry her. I boarded the marriage train and entered a Master's program in social work.

It was a quantum leap in in development between longing for a life I did not have and now having a multi-dimensional one. Unfortunately, this new life came with tumult. Be careful what you wish for!

CHAPTER 7

FALSE STARTS BUT NO DISQUALIFICATIONS IN MY RACE FOR LOVE

The title of this chapter is a running metaphor that describes my impulse to throw my heart in the laps of my love interests before there existed a reasonable basis to commit my heart to these women. In my haste to shrink my commitment timetable, I condemned my poor heart to be discarded on some scrap heap by a disillusioned would-be-heartthrob. When a runner jumps the starter's gun, the starter shoots his pistol a second time to suspend the race. The runners reassemble at the starting line and the guilty party is given a second chance to race. If he jumps the gun a second time, he is disqualified. It is fortunate that love does not work the same way. I did run the risk that the race official in my head would get fed up and ban me for life from racing for love. Fortunately, he or she recognized that I was trying in earnest and never totally lost patience with me.

For many years I permitted powerful, unconscious and wishful scripts to control my destiny. This meant that instead of recognizing when a love interest was a bad fit for me, I simply took artistic liberties and worked them over in my imagination to fit my needs. The result was that my love life was a romance novel with more sequels than the Star Wars franchise. Unfortunately, to para-phrase a very forward thinking psychoanalytic mind of the 20th Century, Harold Searles, my hopes to make fantasies realities were "relentless."

"Reality" back then was a painful rock in my shoe that I pre-ferred to ignore as if waiting for some parent figure to notice I was limping and remove it for me. Paradoxically, the rock eventually made it so painful to walk under my own power that at some point, when the wished-for parent figure did not arrive on my doorstep, I could not ignore the intolerable suffering. In turn, this develop-ment opened my eyes in recognition I had the choice to find a bench, take off my shoe, and remove the irritant.

What were the race officials thinking? Were they accepting bribes from some anonymous patron saint of mine looking to fix the outcome of these races and eventually crown me the winner? Or maybe, seen through a paranoid lens, these were not saints but devils, getting their kicks by keeping me in the race so they could delight watching me fall on my face in love over and over again. My wishful script was designed to erase the necessity of accepting responsibility for a self and a life that was damaged and flawed. My story's plot had me losing myself in merger with a perfect love ob-ject. This love was to validate and make real for me some comely image of myself, and offer me maternal provisions only my worst nightmare of a woman would in truth ever consent to provide.

Several perfectly nice and decent women became unwitting cast members in my soap operas and were hurt by their involve-ments. Fortunately, they took themselves seriously enough to get out early. I am relieved to reflect on the fact that it did not take many of them more than a few months to figure out that they were dealing with a man-child, at which point they cut bait. The dam-age to these love interests was no more than the equivalent of a mild-to-severe hamstring strain for a runner, the type that leaves you sidelined for a couple weeks with no lasting ill effects. Soon it was as if this temporary setback never happened.

I did not mean to break women's hearts. Well, maybe I was indeed taking revenge on my mother in what were unconscious cases of mistaken identities. I truly convinced myself that I was an honorable guy ready and able to choose a life partner. In truth, I wanted to have my cake and to eat it too. That was, to act out childish wishes to not be held accountable for my shameless words and actions. I might have had my cake and eaten it too for short stints but in the long run regretted such immediate gratifications. These empty emotional calories did the equivalent of messing up my entire digestive tract. It would be years before I broke this defensive habit and relinquished these immature fantasies of love.

Early on in their lives my parents were hardwired with a manu-facturer's warning that replacing the original parts could result in electrical shorts, fires, or system shutdowns. These hardwired patterns were of the self-pitying kind that left them looking for handouts from those to whom they imagined life had been much kinder, making these people stand-ins for the siblings who had been favored by their parents. The family myth was that absent such traumas we all would have been stars in our own right. This unfairness meant it was only fair that we be exempt from the rules of fair play, mutual respect and consideration. We "deserved a break." Those who were not victims of trauma and were free to pursue their dreams owed us get-out-of-jail-free cards that would permit us to pass Go and collect whatever.

If I suffered with a Peter Pan complex, my parents felt cursed by a Cinderella complex. Such dynamics mirrored my failed at-tempts at love. I would pursue a love interest expecting handouts and then, when I was slapped on the wrist, I would feel victimized, seeking pity from my support systems for having been so mistreat-ed. I remained crazy-glued for some time to the idea that unless

I rescued my parents from their miserable, self-alienated lives, I deserved to suffer along with them, and so I did. Unfortunately, I tried not to do so alone.

I went as perilously far with this theme as to conflate my usefulness to my parents with my valued identity. This state of affairs produced a chronic uneasiness linked to the completely implausible idea that they could wake up one morning and lay me off, no longer requiring my labors as a child. This was a big existential problem for me, not having yet developed the capacity to sustain a worthwhile identity independent of serving their interests. The fear of non-existence or being alone with myself, with them turning their backs on me, was my ultimate terror. As crazy as this might sound to you, even the psychic equivalents of torturous treatment made me count for something to them, which was preferable to counting for nothing.

It was my quest to be useful that invigorated my pursuit of love. I wished for these "alpha" women to fall in love with my capacity for sensitive attunement to their needs, see my potential and act as my life coaches. What I can admit now that I could not have then was that I sought to recreate the hypnotic appeal of basking in the light of my mother's drooling adoration. In the first flushes of infatuation with these women, I luxuriated in associations to my mother treating me as if I were some royal child. I would throw myself at such women, telling myself I loved them and believing they owed it to me to love me back. I worked feverishly to seduce them with my over-estimated emotional intelligence and willingness to please. My hope was to leave them feeling indebted to reciprocate in kind.

The anatomy of these short-lived affairs continued to play out the Oedipal drama that was still festering in my psyche. Was there a way to replace Dad in Mom's heart without being overwhelmed by Mom's needy nature? Was there a way to move past the need for this father on whose grave I longed to do a touchdown dance? Could I live down vanquishing him in the coliseum of love and live with having the blood of his crushed ego all over my hands?

My older brother's response to an impinging and unreliable home environment was to become a precocious, self-sufficient island who cut himself off from his feelings. His overly intellectualized nature (my family's version of *Star Trek's* Mr. Spock) freed him to bolt and get married when circumstances permitted on or around his 21st birthday. The rest of us were enmeshed with each other and fed each other's false sense of self-importance to compensate for how little we thought of ourselves and took ourselves seriously. Our short-sighted and ill-fated dependencies were the equivalents of junkies without recovery networks and abstinence strategies asking their drug suppliers to support their best clients by not selling drugs to them anymore.

You might call my love relationships prior to meeting Sue, in May of 1988, experimental auditions for the role of husband opposite women on the stage of their real-life ambitions. It is obvious to me in ways it was not at the time that my auditions lacked integrity. They were half-hearted and unconvincing testimony to my unpreparedness to cross the divide between play acting and the heart-felt commitments required to inhabit the role of husband and eventually father. Each time a love interest delivered the message that I had not made the final cut, a state of dejection and grief seized me in the immediate aftermath. Meanwhile, a dissonant and barely audible voice in the deep recesses of my emotional gut let out a sigh of relief, as if a potentially back-breaking burden had been lifted from my narrow and unmuscular shoulders. I can readily say with confidence that no disclaimers on my part controverted the truth that I had induced these women to experience and react to my "cold feet." For me to own my cold feet was to own shameful appendages that I was certain to belittle myself for. So I turned passive fears of rejection into active initiatives to spare myself the fulfillment of my worst fears. Oh how my mother modeled victimhood as virtuous!

What distinguished my audition for Sue from the previous ones was a sincere shift of intention. This time I was prepared to close the deal, or at least I convinced myself this was the case. Sue zealously and unwaveringly maintained that my self-duplicity, which hurt her in the long run, was a cold and calculated ruse to exploit her for my self-centered ends. This recurrent theme cut both ways and so deep as to make it impossible for our betrayals of each other to be forgiven. We were two people not unfamiliar with acts of betrayal at the hands of trusted family members. Sue could not fathom that what looked like a duck and quacked like the ducks of her youth were not quite the ducks remembered through a youthful lens.

My best take is that unprocessed and error-laden interpretations of family dynamics were carried over to me and distorted her perceptions of my behaviors, to our mutual detriment. This was not another dabble for me in affairs of the heart. Marriage, ready or not was the goal. For years my semi-reclusive state holed up inside a studio apartment no larger than a claustrophobic berth on a cruise ship did the job to protect this wounded soul from further harm. This lifestyle, however, was not a proving ground to learn the intricate ebbs and flows of interdependent marital relations. As I became more adept at putting my past in perspective as a beginning frame of reference for making sense of the present moment, my studio refuge looked and felt more like a quasi-sensory deprivation chamber. Stretches of time alone fraught with a dearth of human contact began to figuratively drive me crazy. The single life for a guy who craved attention had become so boring as to barely have a pulse.

This was a sign of emotional health. Dr. G's examination of my head, a very slow fix, was paying dividends. How poignantly ironic that in the 21st century we dig ourselves into holes of debt so deep to earn professional licenses, yet one can still purchase a marriage license without any qualifications to lovingly promote the health and welfare of another.

In 1988, I was virtually clueless about how to negotiate emotional space with a partner and ensure that the tent we put up for our mutual protection did not collapse under duress from the inside out. If histories of human relations do repeat themselves, then it was not a stretch for me to infer that Sue learned early on to apologize for breathing too much air if a parent greedily sucked all the air out of the room. This dynamic among others did not bode well for sharing what each of us needed in fairly equal measure to thrive. I took a cue from my observations, and when Sue identified herself with such a parent, I breathed sparingly. I flew down the aisle by the seat of my pants and could not stay more than a micro second with the flashes of insight that my ship was still running on some pre-programmed, conflict-avoidant autopilot.

Conflict in my household of origin was like border tensions between North Korea and South Korea. Every perceived boundary violation committed by one parent against the other was due cause for me to hold my breath in dread of a potential escalation of hostilities. From what Sue reported to me, her natal family was likewise a system where diplomacy took a holiday when conflicts erupted. Had our parents enjoyed secure attachments to each other, Sue and I might have had a fighting chance to stay together. We were in truth not even a long shot to stay together a high stakes gambler would risk.

Trauma held my parents' imaginations hostage. Their imaginations were factories outfitted to reproduce nightmares. So they avoided conflict at all costs, until the gauges on their tanks of self-respect registered empty. Until that point was reached, as if on cue one spouse laid down on the floor so that the other felt free to run over the prostate form of the other in pursuit of his or her desired goal.

You will not be surprised to hear that such compulsive and undignified behavior over time made for an over pressurized marital cooker that blew its lid. My parents most days did not dare offer anymore resistance to their designs on each other than Czechoslovakia offered Hitler's forces when they took the country by storm. They both feared staring down the barrel of their historical predictions that each possessed the power to annihilate the self-worth of the other. My parents' narrative framed "doing" as vital and useful. "Being" was a state of quiescence associated with a moribund coma-like state, or suicidal depression. They dreaded that such quiescence might ensue as fallout from conflict. If my parents had not needed each other to hold their breath so the other could have breathing room, their marriage in this era might have had half, a third or maybe even a quarter of the shelf life it had. All that is comfortable and familiar is not healthy, happiness or growth promoting.

Such was my instruction on how to choreograph my half of the marital dance. Yes, I did wishfully think that these dance moves might produce better results with Sue as my partner. If everything in love is timing, then I thought 1988 was well timed for me to go the distance with Sue. My flesh and blood mother still claimed me as her possession, but my power over my own life was as strong as my grip, and I gripped my life more tightly these days. My mother, the martyr, could no longer get to me with tearful refrains like "I'm your mother," which meant it was my duty to drop everything I was doing when she called or else listen to her flagellate herself for failing me by dint of my election to make myself, and not her, the center of my own universe.

Sue knew wholeheartedly that she did not have to worry that she was in competition with my flesh-and-blood mother for sole possession of my heart. She did, however, grossly underestimate the unremitting influence of my inner mother who left me feeling insufficient to satisfy her needs and thus, unworthy of Sue's love. I would withdraw from Sue, worried she would feel about me the way I felt about myself, and such distance activated her longstanding fears of abandonment. Then with steam rising from her head, she would chase after me as if to say: "Don't you think one minute I will let you walk out on me!" Other times, Sue expressed her split ambivalence about me by throwing me out of our apartment. This knee-jerk reaction was reminiscent of my father's worst vitriol hurled at my brother.

So in a perverse way, we were perfect for each other. The woman to win my heart had to be comfortable running her own life and mine as well. Sue's qualifications in this regard were impeccable: They were superior to those of anyone previously who had given me a second look or vice versa.

I worked very hard over the course of our marriage to become more self-sufficient and demonstrate greater respect for Sue's needs. Still, until the day arrived much later on that I felt squarely in charge of my life, every choice I made felt like a concession extracted from me against my free will by internal or external forces superior to this will. Sue, for no fault of her own, was squarely behind the eight ball of my sullen and irritated demeanor that conveyed the following message: "I don't have the right to choose my destiny but you expect me to honor your self-interest and make more sacrifices in the process?" Yes, go ahead and say it: "Why didn't you grow up?" I was not ready. Her split ambivalence complemented mine. "Please run my life when I need you to and when I do not wish for this, I will blame you for me choosing to not run my own life."

Sue eventually came to grips with the reality that, way too often, the voice she heard was the voice of an over-matched little boy, and the person I spoke to was not her but a suffocating parent of yore. My over-conditioned, reactive survival strategy was to regress to earlier emotional states when my safety and security felt threatened. The unconscious belief I clung to for dear life was that my wife would feel too guilty to throw this child out into the street. What left me so forlorn was that I functioned in so many spheres as a capable adult and yet felt so small and incompetent both at work and home.

If you put a water gun to Sue's head, even she would admit I grew significantly between the time we met and the time we went our separate ways. What still counted way too much, absent a reliable mindful lens, was that my reality was dictated by how I had learned to feel and think about myself. These thoughts and feelings hijacked my abilities to make fair and balanced performance evaluations of myself. Often confused and self-doubting, I chalked my accomplishments up to luck, divine intervention, or the good offices of those who wielded the greatest influence over me, past and present.

Sue took me much more seriously than I was ready to take myself, and this was a very sad error in judgment on her part. She provided a much needed impetus of ambition and industrious energy that was just what the doctor ordered for me to get my vocational life on track. She was up to the task of cheering me on and telling me I could do this and I could do that, like go to graduate school and develop a private practice. Sue was literally able to do back flips, in heels no less, while exhorting me on from the sidelines. She insisted that if I loved her, then I would meet her timetables for such attainments with the precision of predictions for sunrises and sunsets. Unbeknownst to both of us at the time, her estimates were short sighted on the order of the gross miscalculations of the number of years it would take our special forces to hunt down Osama Bin Laden.

Failure to meet her most cherished expectations was prosecuted in a manner that left me feeling as if on trial for a capital offense. Such cross examinations rattled my already rattled nervous system, making it less possible for me to take charge of and integrate the many sides of Sue into a balanced whole. I split and compartmentalized these disparate sides to the detriment of both of us. Since I was not sure which Sue to expect from one moment to the next, justly or not, I stayed away, to Sue's great offense. Stress and vulnerability were a potent combination that shaped my aversion to intimate relations of any kind. My caricatures of Sue as the good and the bad mother ate away at whatever love and respect she once felt towards me.

Children can be repositories of our relentless hopes to fix the damage done to our trust in the universe to provide for us and trust in ourselves to make creative use of these gifts. I have no doubt that, as much progress as I had made in my life, I was depressed over my chances to break the chain of victimization that was the footprint of trauma on my life. My intuition did not disappoint. At this juncture, proactively caring for the infancies of my kids was much easier for me than caring proactively for similar stages of infancy that inhabited me. My kids' early idealization of me buoyed my self-regard. The idea that the miracle of birth and the dawn of unlimited possibilities for these precious lumps of organic clay might rekindle hopes for us to give birth to new possibilities for relating to each other was a pleasant fantasy, and one that was not actualized in our home. What our children did was delay the inevitable dissolution of our marriage until we were both ready. Parenthood was a daily wake up call for me that "playing house," once it included little ones, was very serious business.

Once Jocelyn, my first-born, joined our family, like a house settling into its foundation, I could sense cracks in my denial that if this marriage was not built to last, the good old days of calling such an affair of the heart a false start and then moving on in short order were long behind me. We were stuck with each other, whether we liked it or not, for a stretch of time that was as unbelievable to me as the number of years it took me to write and edit this book.

This sobering idea brought me to treatment with a renewed sense of purpose. My mission was to not recapitulate my parents' miserable marriage. To live with a traumatized brain is to live in a perpetual state of waiting for some memory fragment to drop out of nowhere and seize control of your mental operations. Often patients and therapists speak about such emotional flashbacks as waiting for the other shoe to drop. When such shoes also represent the proliferation of unresolved marital problems in banished states of suspended animation, one never knows, depending on the gravity of the situation, when the sky will begin raining shoes.

Sue painfully and rage-fully pointed out that I was more relaxed and forthcoming with just about anyone except her. In particular I had intimate ties to my shrink, a secure attachment relationship she did not share or have on her own that made my treatment alliance an object of simmering jealousy. Sadly, Sue never admitted as much, so she bristled in futility over this matter. Psychoanalysis and running were the second and third vertices in a triangle that both stabilized our uneasy alliance but also drove a wedge between us.

If I sleepwalked to some degree through my second psychoanalysis it was in part due to the fact that Dr. K succumbed during my thrice-weekly analysis to demands that he admire my free-associations and keep his mouth shut. I dare say he dropped the ball, permitting me to use him exclusively as a psychic mirror in front of which I liked to flex my analytic muscles. Maybe he was so bored by my narcissistic self-involvement that he spent our sessions writing grocery lists or considering how he might conclude his latest professional article. In any case, Dr. K and I repeated what had gone on during my childhood and repeated in my marriage. I wished to be seen as an outlier hoping that such reflections might transform this under achiever into a high achiever. When it did not, I became procrastinator *par excellence* and would filibuster with the best of them to delay having to put up or shut up.

My narcissistic exercises were at the expense of much needed experimentation, discussion, and rehearsal of ways I might relate more effectively to Sue. We spent an inordinate amount of time on the redesign of my psychological interior, and on occasion discussing what it meant that in this moment or that moment that I cast Dr. K in this way or that.

In fairness to this big teddy bear of an intellectual giant, no one in our treatment room possessed the authority to influence Sue to give more credence to my perspective on matters. Dr K did meet with Sue alone in the eleventh hour of our marriage upon her request, with my blessings, but our marital script had been commissioned a long time ago with only one conceivable ending. Sue was destined to launch me with her powerful right leg end-over-end through the uprights and into the section occupied by divorced husbands.

Through this period, my fundamental oversight was that, rather than learning to take the reins of my own life, my deepest wish was still that Sue would become a more benign boss. To what degree Sue would have seized the reins no matter how little or great was my resistance to sharing authority and responsibility with her is impossible to know. What I recall was that she regarded expressions of my autonomy with trepidation-fueled aggression, as if apprehensive that my actions might cause her brain to sound its alarms and plunge her into reliving the hostile chaos of her youth. The day I began to assert myself was the day that our battles escalated in paranoid intensity.

Call it conceit, grandiosity, denial, fear, or whatever else you wish, I wanted desperately to save my marriage. There was a laundry list of behaviors my wife wanted me to change. As much as I was hurt and angry by what I considered to be a dearth of loving acceptance, I persisted with my wish to singlehandedly change how she felt about me by earnestly working to satisfy her. In my estimation, I made a yeoman's efforts to transition from my wife's man-child helper to her partner. Still, in her estimation my efforts consistently fell short of a passing grade. Curiously, my actions were forever too little or too late. Furthermore, Sue's preferred manner of asking was to complain after the fact about what I should have known to do but was not asked to do. I will admit that I was much better at reading my own mind than I was reading Sue's and often confused the two to her mounting chagrin. During these episodes, I felt as if I were being set up to be slapped on the wrist.

Eventually, our marriage like, a hastily designed and shoddily built house made of substandard construction materials, started to crumble. Sue began to internalize the blame I slowly would not accept as my cross to bear. She became depressed and began looking for the exit door. The end of my marriage was a gathering storm, and I was one of those folks who do not evacuate their homes no matter what. As I write this, I am struck by how much this was in keeping with my parent's natures. Neither would have left each other under any circumstances.

As a departure from their norms, I began to think that the end was in sight, a sign of growing ego strength for me and a source of hope that I might survive my separation anxieties and reconstitute my identity as a single parent. Previously, neither of us could tolerate the other's unhappiness, because we could not separate or individuate from such unhappiness. Now with the fruits of our collective futility a forgone conclusion, survival dictated that we each see ourselves as distinct and separate from the other's unhappiness with each other.

The context of our marriage was not unlike today's politics in which combatants wage wars on multiple platforms, fluidly shifting alliances so that you cannot tell the good guys from the bad guys. The actors employ sophisticated weaponry including cyber-sabotage and information theft, economic sanctions, robot technology, airpower, traditional ground skirmishes, and guerrilla warfare. Not unlike them, Sue and I engaged in hot and cold wars around issues of power and control, money, love, and physical and emotional space. Yet, as it pertained to our kids, we could put aside our mutual enmity and ally effectively, like the U.S. government partnering with Iraqi rebels against their common enemy, the Islamic State.

Unfortunately, only mutual love would have saved us, and it was conspicuously absent. Our mutual inability to idealize and love each other as whole, flawed people became an intolerable state of affairs that ate away at our own self-regard and the regard for each other like sulfuric acid. Have you seen what sulfuric acid does to exposed flesh? These feelings were unbelievably corrosive, and as our marriage moved closer to its termination, I was prone to bouts of fearful desperation.

Running was a form of self-care that helped me hold onto myself as an entity worth caring for. Although I ran four to five days a week outdoors for no more than 20 to 30 minutes, even this required a certain amount of spousal coordination, especially with two small children in the house. As much as Sue recognized that I was running away from the marital tensions when I worked out, she said, but never meant, "Do it on your own time." Our quid pro quo was that Sue did not refuse to watch the kids when I wished to run, and I forfeited, like it or not, the right to say no when she needed me to watch the kids so she could run errands. Sue seemed to understood intuitively that I depended on running to modulate an over-stimulated sympathetic nervous system, which, when over excited, left me with a substandard track record of success on my own.

My days as a small apartment dweller were about to make a comeback. Given my unceasing desire to be cared for in ways no one, including Sue had ever satisfied, I clung to the wish that my penchant to punish myself for Sue's rejection of me might be a cause for her concern. She would not want a depressed ex-husband caring for our children now would she?

Other than my apprenticeship as a mindfulness engineer in psychoanalysis, running was my ego's best weapon and last defense against being overrun by the demands of the real world on the one hand and getting caught on the other in the crossfire between instinctual desires for immediate gratification and my heavy-handed law enforcer, my conscience. My difficulties in keeping the internal peace most certainly were played out between Sue and myself. This internal state of affairs exacerbated the conflicts between two spouses already at loggerheads with each other. One day in the distant future, running would enhance and no longer compensate for my deficient regulatory capacities. When that day arrived, I would more effectively see and resolve my confusion between the past and the present and retain my freedom to choose my path moving forward. For now, running was as much my mistress as it had been in the past. One might say given the celibate state of affairs in our bedroom, bedding down with a mistress named Nike or Reebok was the lesser of two evils than bedding down with one named Barbara, Cathy or Donna.

By the time our daughters were 5 and 2 ½, my take is that Sue was ready to kill three birds with the one stone of divorce: She rid herself of a husband she had systematically devalued, took unconscious revenge on the image of her father who had abandoned her, and fulfilled her mother's implicit mandate to join her as a long-suffering divorced mother.

One evening in 1998, Sue informed me that she was filing for divorce. I see now that she had to be the one to leave. If I had walked out on her, as her father had done when she was young, I would never have lived down reopening that narcissistic injury. The fact that her announcement took me by surprise had to be chalked up to my God complex. I was not ready for it to happen, so I commanded that it should not be.

Interestingly, the end of our marriage at about the 10-year mark was one year short of the 11-year mark in Sue's life when her mother evicted her father. For all intents and purposes, any fathering he gave her ceased once he left the house. In other words, when it proved impossible for me to shape up sufficiently to repair the traumatic wounds inflicted by Sue's father, it appeared to me that she was destined to take revenge on me.

Suddenly, I was a divorced father. Outside of work, Sue had been the hub of the wheel of my existence. With the divorce the spokes that emanated from it ceased to exist. I am referring to our home in the suburbs, our neighbors who now kept their distance as if I had been recently paroled for discharging a firearm with intent to kill, as well as my in-laws whose informal adoption of me into their family was revoked the day my wife announced to them she was leaving me.

Just about everyone takes sides in acrimonious separations. This one was very civil, while equally acrimonious. The final nail in the coffin for our marriage that caused my deepest wound was the forfeiture of daily opportunities to spend time with my kids. Allison has no recollection of her father living in the same house with her. Jocelyn and I were once inseparable, forged in part by her mother's business travel schedule that took her all over the world. Our relationship would never be the same, even though we continued to love each other from a distance. It would be a decade before I stopped lamenting the fact I missed my kids.

Sue and I had gotten together when I was 34-years-old. When I moved out on December 4, 1999, I was 45 years of age. It felt as if I had lost 11 years of my life or maybe more accurately, my mind spent the majority of those 11 years everywhere except in the moment lived. As I would throughout my life, I turned again to running to survive losses. Through running, I recaptured my fond associations to a youthful past and found in the continuity in this relationship a healing salve for this ruptured marriage. As long as I could still run even at 45, maybe this failed marriage did not disqualify me from reentering the race for true love.

CHAPTER 8

LAST RITES FOR DAD AND MY RITE OF SUCCESSION TO THE THRONE OF MY LIFE

My father was diagnosed with colon cancer in his 86th year. A coroner's report might have listed this disease as causation for the cessation of his life. Yet, if we are to define life as the capacity to thrive as opposed to merely surviving, my father's terminally morbid condition had little to do with disease processes in his colon. It predated the expression of this disease by the better part of a century. My father's psyche never made peace with the large traumas of death by starvation that haunted his family during the near economic collapse that was the Great Depression, or the desperate, frantic call to take arms against the megalomania of Adolph Hitler whose ambition was to incinerate Jews like my father into extinction. These traumas with a capital "T" piled on top of the accumulation of traumas with a small "t," the insults and injuries to his developing selfhood by caregivers who knew not that they were murdering my father's zest for life. What my father could never articulate is left for this chapter to describe.

After Dad's diagnosis with colon cancer, I do not recall his physician broaching with us the subject of the moral calculus of prolonging his life, a life whose sleepy lethargy was infrequently punctuated by a bowel movement or, on a very good day, the opportunity to flirt with the floor nurse when she arrived to check his vital signs. The surgeon had no idea that my father had been sitting idly, waiting for nature to take its course. Once neurological degeneration had robbed him of the command of his legs, it likewise robbed him of his interest in the world. We knew that the surgeon's scalpel could perhaps remove the diseased tissue from my father's colon but could do nothing for Dad's bitter regrets of having wasted his life.

Looking back, the decision to operate on my father's colon was nonsensical. Why did it happen?   I will not completely rule out the chance that my unconscious desire to exact sadistic revenge played a part. A less damning and thus preferred interpretation was that I, as little brother, deferred to my big brother on decisions regarding the health and welfare of our parents. I had learned to over-value Peter's analytic abilities, just as he had learned to under-value mine.

Earlier in life I deferred to my brother to preserve his love and support, which were once indispensable. Now such a dynamic was an archaic vestige of a bygone era. I have zero doubts that both of us carried his role in my life as surrogate father way beyond the point at which either of us felt more often than not, burdened by it.

With the decision to operate on a patient that was by most measures beyond salvation, Peter spoke openly to me about wanting a clear conscience: He wanted to know that he had done everything for our parents he could to prolong and improve the quality of their lives. There was no doubt about his honorable intentions. Peter, for example, had been the driving force for my parents to purchase a home in a senior community and then spearheaded the initiative to get my parents situated in a clean and well-run nursing home when they could no longer care for themselves.

Notwithstanding his well-deserved kudos for the aforementioned accomplishments, reason went out the window when we opted to remove the cancerous section of my father's colon. For my own part, just shy of 50, I remained exquisitely apprehensive of him dying, killing off all hope of me or anyone else miraculously rescuing him from himself. In my most imaginatively ruinous moments "survivor guilt" became a relentlessly cruel internal persecutor, doling out my just desserts for having allowed my father to die as he had lived, miserably unhappy. What kind of a son would sit by and not protect his father from being mugged by some internal hoods? So I despaired at the idea of my father dying without achieving redemption, thus in turn rendering me unworthy of absolution.

There is an old saying in the world of professional sports: You let sleeping dogs lie. The worst thing a superior team can do when it has its hands on the other team's jugular is to make the sleeping team angry. Well, we did the equivalent by opening up our father and inflicting upon him a painful surgery. Dad had checked out on living some time before that and would have probably gone quietly into the night had the surgeon not left him writhing in pain after surgery. Now when he awoke it was like old times. He was irascible, inconsolable, and intent on airing his grievances about the short shrift he had received in life. Lucky for us, our father could not catch his breath for very long and so his venomous diatribe lacked endurance.

Once a breathing tube was inserted down my father's throat he was effectively muzzled, and we could then stop holding our breaths. None of us could listen to him without wanting to scream. The dying man in front of us was the principal architect of our unhealed traumas. Neither of us would have admitted this at the time, but our family resemblances went way beyond an inventory of physical characteristics. This was a room of people who stubbornly refused to shed their status as victims. Consequently, no one was about to let bygones be bygones. There would be no efforts at reconciliation or peace-making among the living in this room. Even in his unconscious state, we were both too fearful and self-righteous to bare our souls to him.

On Thursday, September 22, it was time to pull the plug on my father's artificial lungs and let nature take its course. In fact, the hospital administration rushed to this decision and we were not permitted the opportunity to be by my father's bedside to offer a final goodbye. For all his failings Dad was very affectionate to me and vice versa, and I felt sad to have been deprived of the opportunity to convey my love to my father in the only manner I was comfortable, with a hug and a kiss.

In what felt like a shameless acquiescence to the hospital "bottom line," my father's body was spirited to the morgue before we had time to offer a dignified farewell. So there we were, my brother, my wheelchair-bound mother brought by ambulette from her nursing home, and myself in this macabre setting in the bowels of the hospital. We were summoned to identify my father's body. The image of my father's dead body seized with rigor mortis, his jaw agape and his complexion ghost-like reminded me of the art and science of taxidermy on display in the Museum of Natural History. As true to life as these stuffed animals appear to be, their eyes are portals to empty shells. The spirits of these life forms have without mistake checked out of their corporeal suites.

My mother let loose a blood curdling scream that told the tale of the incomprehensible loss of a 62-year-long marriage. No matter that my parents were at each other's throats more often than not. The primal scream of this inconsolable newly widowed woman underscored what we all knew at the level of heart and soul. They were inseparable. If Mom had a say in the matter, they would not be separated for very long.

One of my regrets in writing this book was the requirement that I revisit this experience. If there was any good that came out of me being present for this grisly identification, it was proof positive I was slowly but surely becoming someone who "showed up" and could be counted on to handle what life had to dish out to me. Though I was not yet running toward my dreams, I was no longer running away from challenges, either.

What happened next, inside the bowels of the hospital, was the most unexpected tender mercy imaginable. A light bulb went off in my head. *What if,* I pondered, *death accomplished for Dad what psychoanalysis had not yet done for me? What if Dad's soul that had been so abused during his lifetime was now once again restored to its natural identity as an object of reverence?*

For one of the few times perhaps since my father's drunken laps around a New Year's Eve buffet table back in the mid 60's, I held him in my imagination as ebulliently free. Dad seemed lighter than air dancing on some puffy cloud, as if his morbid cynicism was replaced by gleeful awe. The father who now held center stage in my imagination had reconnected to and was celebrating the inherent worth and value of his essence. Now in my mind's wishful eye, Dad owned the spacious mindfulness that would allow him to forgive me for being human. If he no longer needed fixing and was one with his divine origins, I could not imagine any encumbrances on him loving me. I saw my father as I always wished him to be, smiling down on me with acceptance, love, and admiration.

The morning of Dad's funeral I went for a run and felt his presence in perfect rhythm with my strides. A delicious calm came over me that I had only known after intense workouts or moments of intensely focused creative flow. This morning was different. I felt my father's spirit as simply being with me and for me, without any pressures on me to inflate his ego, interminably losing air like a tire punctured by a nail. The joy and serenity that surrounds those who do not feel alone, are not afraid of what is coming their way, and feel they are competent and lovable, seemed to be everywhere and nowhere.

In attendance at the funeral were two embattled and embittered families, too exhausted from the stresses living decade upon decade with mood, anxiety, and personality disorders to rip each other apart. The rift with my first cousins had become a geriatric Jewish variation on the Hatfield's and McCoy's, but by the time my father died, the fight was tired. Many of the principal combatants, my cousins' parents and grandparents on either side were either dead, losing their marbles sufficiently to forget what they were angry about, or unable to sustain an argument for more than thirty seconds without needing a nap.

The rift with my father's younger brother had likewise exceeded some unwritten statute of limitations on internecine strife. This uncle, the lone college-educated professional of that nuclear family, had single handedly kept my father employed in clerical capacities for decades after blood poisoning ended his career as a printer. During that time, my father had complained to anyone and everyone about the environmental discomforts of working in a warehouse setting, compounded by the undue emotional stress of being forced to deal with liberties taken by adult children in a family-owned business who flouted with impunity standards of fairness and decency. As a result, my uncle spent his adult years miffed and mystified that my father could meet his largesse with such ingratitude. My uncle felt so disgusted with my father's shameless and burdensome expectations that he pretty much stopped inviting us to family gatherings at his house. Sadly, the other siblings followed suit. Yet on this day, my Uncle Bernie stood shoulder-to-shoulder with me at the funeral weeping uncontrollably as I thanked him for guaranteeing my family a middle-class lifestyle. We both had unsuccessfully longed for my father's appreciation of what we had given him.

It was up to me to give my father's eulogy. My mother, had she not been in cognitive decline, might have chosen to deliver this. But she was not in full possession of her faculties. She had struggled so mightily to hide from the truth of my father's impending death that at no point did it dawn on her to share with me the coincidental passing of my father's elder sister Ruth two weeks ear-lier. Here I was thanking Ruth's daughter Elaine for paying her re-spects, whom by the way I had not seen in a dog's age, only to step in an absolute humongous pile of dog shit, ignorantly asking her: "Was your mother not well enough to join you today?" It is a pretty fair conclusion that if someone is dead, she is not well enough to travel. I did not realize it was humanly possible to shove my foot that far down my throat. If I could have dug a makeshift hole, I would have taken refuge in it as in an unmarked grave. I made a bee's line to the open ambulette where inside my mother sat shaded from the hot sun, waiting for the graveside service to com-mence. My mother spied the incredulous look on my face and shot me back a child-like guilty glance as if she had been caught with her hand in the cookie jar and was about to be sent to her room. I started with: "Mom you have to be kidding." Then I thought about the absurdity of trying to reason with her and fell silent. Nothing else needed to be said between us.

My brother, as well, was incapable of delivering my father's eu-logy, as there were no more than three people in the world he trusted to care for his fragile emotions. The first was his paternal grandfather who died in 1961, the second was Aunt Naomi who died in 1989, and the third was his wife Lisa (whom in 2016 cel-ebrated 47 years of marriage with him). Peter was prone to para-noid interpretations of others' actions, making him self-conscious over what he regarded as shameful aspects of his nature. Even had he been more comfortable baring his soul, his revulsion for dis-honesty toward those he despised would have rendered it impos-sible for him to pay a tribute to our departed father.

So here I was, the most logical candidate to eulogize my fa-ther. Heck, I was the kid born to write Hallmark greeting cards: I had maintained the hope that if "being me" did not work to win friends and admirers, then maybe fawning over others with my literary flair would do the trick. My only expectation was that you liked me for all my pandering.

My eulogy that morning was intended to meet a handful of objectives. First and foremost, it was my intention to make amends in a very personal and public fashion for not having adequately honored my father's contributions to our family during his life-time. It was also my intention to cast my father as a reluctant and a damaged hero, but a hero nonetheless. He was an unsung hero as a working child to a family devastated by financial collapse, and later to a country at war. It was time for me to stand up for the val-ues I had been clarifying for years in therapy. It was time to dignify a life that, while causing me pain, had paradoxically helped shape my calling as a psychoanalyst, thus paving the route that would ultimately lead to joy and serenity.

Underpinning my noble intentions was a desperate yearning to not reach the end of my life feeling ripped off, as had my fa-ther. I was nearly 50 years old, and opportunities to rewrite this narrative felt like they were slipping through my fingers. With this eulogy of my father, I tried to resurrect the secure attachment fig-ure I believed I needed to move forward. Like Obama speaking at the 2004 Democratic Convention, this was my coming out party in which I was to lay out my ambitious visions for change. My platform was simply to reclaim power over my own life and hopefully invite those in attendance to reclaim power over their lives. I hoped they would see through my eyes the overlooked and under-appreciated efforts of my beleaguered father and apply this perspective as an analgesic to their jaundiced narratives. I was not alone among the mourners in attendance who had blown my father's hurtful deeds and miscast aims out of proportion to the harm internalized. If I were to move forward in my life I felt it imperative, as the next gen-eration of cemetery plots were being paid off (which would have included my own had I not opted for cremation), to cease to let any internal or external authority kill off my growing autonomous authority over my life. I set the record straight that morning and damn anybody who did not have a sense of humor about my errors in historical accuracy.

In the days after my father died, I flew high in a short-lived state of manic bliss. Yet, shortly afterwards, the return of an inescapable felt sense of mortality brought with it a sense of urgency to fulfill longstanding goals. The movie, "The Bucket List" starring Jack Nicholson and Morgan Freeman, looked at how, when the going gets terminal, the terminally ill get going on living life to its fullest. Well, I was not terminally ill at the time, but I undeniably carried a terminal prognosis. Although the movie did not debut until 2007, I was ripe for such a vehicle to light a fire under me to put a creative stamp on my life.

Two years prior to formally creating my bucket list, I had articulated the following lifetime achievements as worthy of my time and attention: 1) Get married and develop a secure and loving adult attachment; and 2) Write a book to chronicle my spiritual journey. This book was intended to use my relationship to running to illustrate the inter-subjective nature of relationships. A large network of relationships helped me conceive, incubate, give birth to, and mature my mindful self. Within the context of these dynamic exchanges of information and energy that changed all of us, running molded my character, and I in turn changed it by how I altered my perspectives on this activity.

Both items on my bucket list required a disciplined opening up of myself and there was no way for me to create space without loosening attachments to old identifications and holding fast as the energies released made for temporary states of chaos. It was imperative that I learn to fight against the pull of worry-bound apparitions that left me frozen by archaic fears.

Often when I find myself being sucked up by unconscious forces, I summon the image of the boxer Sugar Ray Leonard in his

1981 fight against Thomas Hearns. Trailing in points before the 13th round, Leonard's trainer Angelo Dundee said to him, "You're blowing it kid!" That was all Sugar Ray needed to hear to awaken to and break a pattern of engagement with Hearns that was destining Sugar Ray to be on the losing end of this match. Leonard came out in the 13th round as if a man possessed and hit Hearns like a windmill in hyper drive. In the 14th round, Leonard was declared the winner by technical knockout as the referee stopped the fight to protect the helpless Hearns from serious injury.

Distance running had trained me to be a disciplined soldier fighting at cross-purposes, both for and against the causes of others. Now in the aftermath of my father's death and funeral, I discovered a new kind of running. This running was for myself. It was not about enduring fears of life and death but about expressing the power of my being. During this period, I turned to sprinting.

I have heard it said (and have found it true) that when the student is ready, the teacher will appear. Such was the case of my introduction to vascular surgeon Irving Dardik. He was the subject of Dr. Roger Lewin's 2005 biography titled "Making Waves: Irving Dardik and his Superwave Theory." This biography captured my imagination. I will not touch with a 10-foot pole Dr. Dardik's claims that by regulating heart rhythms he could heal illnesses that continue to baffle the medical community. What I will tell you is that "interval training," my application of his theory for cultivating optimal wellness, has been indispensable to the growth of my capacities to perform creative work.

Once I adopted interval training as my preferred exercise of choice – short, high-intensity sprints with full recoveries between bursts of exertion – my resistance to the common cold and bouts of flu went through the roof. There was a big difference between four to six colds per year that might last several weeks and perhaps one to two colds per year that were one week in duration and did not interfere with anything I did. I found myself able to develop increasingly greater capacities to perform work without undue fatigue. This new paradigm of running improved dramatically my resilience in the face of all manner of stresses, physical and emotional. Furthermore, I was only running four days per week and could complete a workout that included a regimen of stretching and a shower in 45 minutes.

I worked with a patient whose accelerated breathing during exercise triggered a somatosensory memory of childhood abuse. Until we were able to reintegrate this symptom into the patient's life narrative, any activity that led to hard breathing would activate false alarms in his brain and he could find himself in a full-scale panic. In keeping with this theme of the "body as mind," I discovered while sprinting that if my mind was not relaxed, focused and free of threatening preoccupations, I ran the risk that tension-producing mental content might push my muscles beyond the limits of their capacity to do work and land me on the disabled list.

Through this realization, I learned to use my sprinting to practice mindful meditation. I had to commit myself to a mindful, caring and concerned focus on what I was doing to avoid the traumatic muscular injuries that came with the territory of highly ballistic movements. And this mindfulness helped me hone my capacities to relax and stay regulated. Consequently, my training now enhanced my capacities to be mindful, and I used running to take me out of self-defeating unconscious modes of operating to reassert executive control over my life. By anchoring myself in the moment, emptying my mind of worldly concerns and disciplining my focus on the movement at hand, I programmed myself to more readily stay present and to remove myself from those timeless abysses that are emotional flashbacks. In addition, if my muscles were holding memories with the potential to trigger mental disorganization, there was nothing like maximal sprints to discharge these energies and help me reestablish contact with my executive functioning.

I did not at the time understand how much I was programming my mind for success in life outside of running by improving my flexibility, mobility, efficiency and ease of movement, coordination, rhythm, power, and immunity to illness and injury. No matter what adversity I faced in my life, four days per week without fail, I was out running sprints. This activity helped me to build and sustain a coherent identity even during periods of fragmentation when I related to myself as "only this" or "only that," instead of a coordinated and integrated collection of personality units. What went up had to learn how to come down safely as well, and sprinting trained me not only to quickly and efficiently shift into higher gears but also how to trust myself to flexibly downshift with ease, efficiency and grace. This activity helped me learn how to regulate my nervous system and experientially commit to memory its felt nuances. These workouts were pennies in the bank account of my self-confidence and self-esteem as I learned to go the distance, one day at a time.

Whereas in my younger years more was better and too much was not nearly enough, leading me into a target zone of overuse injuries and illnesses, now I understood that rest and recovery were indispensable to maintaining healthy and growth-promoting biorhythms. Sleep, relaxation and a healthy diet progressively became higher priorities, as they were indispensable to the growth of new coordinating and integrating neural networks.

A shift from mindless reveries while running long, slow distance, to mindful responsive attunement to the language of my body was an experiential seminar on how to heal my traumas from the "bottom up," as well as from the "top down," by cognitively reframing my experiences. I credit experts and gifted teachers such as Richard Chefetz, the author of "Intensive Psychotherapy for Persistent Dissociative Processes" for teaching me how to isolate, track and modify physical sensations as a means to keep my observing lens online and stave off the return of full-blown dissociated traumatic states. These are commonly referred to as emotional flashbacks of sorts. The more I accepted trauma as a constituent part of my mental palate, the more effectively I managed these self-states. In turn, the more vigorously and proactively I pursued efforts to control the potential damage they inflicted on my equanimity. What were once triggers for vicious downward spirals were now objects of mindful attention employed to motivate to positive upward cycles. Success in life became a function of making incremental strides in the recognition and neutralization of traumatic states.

What a glorious picture, right? Well, not quite yet. As I said, learning important life lessons and actually applying these lessons are distinct tasks. And my real-world abilities were about to be tested.

In August of 2000, I accepted a state government job that embedded me in a New England criminal court. By legal statute, I had license to offer my opinion on which nonviolent defendants were eligible for mental health treatment alternatives to incarceration. I drew my clients from a pool of chronically mentally ill, indigent adults whose mental competence was deemed sufficiently impaired to mitigate responsibility for their crimes. For my clients, the degree of difficulty of their path to justice was a negotiation amongst the sitting judge, state prosecutor, defendant's attorney (often a public defender), victim's advocate when indicated, and myself. A fair, balanced and just evaluation was often thrown off kilter by such factors as swollen and stressful dockets, personal dislike of defendants, and a host of society-wide prejudices against the weakest and most vulnerable members of society.

If I learned anything by this time it was that less separates the servants from those they serve than the servants may ever admit to ourselves. To the degree we are aware of these matters and can own them with dignity, respect and compassion determines in large measure how justly we will treat those we serve. We were all dedicated public servants in this jurisdiction doing our absolute best that on some days was not very good. Consequently, my client's diversion from the prison system, a de facto warehouse for the mentally ill, was on any given day anything from a stroll in the park to an Olympic steeplechase event for some who could barely walk under their own power.

I worked under the command of a supervisor I'll call "Sam." Sam was a psychologist-philosopher who could be quite the astute and reflective observer of human nature. He took an interest in me and was as generous with gifts, raises and praise for my creative and intellectual gifts as my father had been stingy. Oh how I idealized him early on! Like my father, Sam was not above bullying those he exercised authority over. Equally so, my observation of Sam more than 10 years removed from our last encounter was that he was acutely vulnerable to anything he might misinterpret as disrespect for his title and authority. Unlike my father, Sam was smart and cunning enough to play clandestine political games with great skill in this non-profit setting. This I assumed was a stratagem consistent with a self-image as a noble warrior. Here was a man whose noble ends justified what struck me to be his "sometimes" disagreeable means.

He was a romantic idealist and in this regard we were two peas in a pod. Unlike my father, his responses were informed by a deep intelligence of what made other people tick, the least of which, I would say to the misfortune of his charges, peers and higher ups, was possessed about himself. To put it another way, I thought Sam exerted powerful influence over others' thoughts and feelings and then misinterpreted their responses as if they were identical to him or his early attachment figures. Often, he was grossly in error.

Sam oscillated between sympathy and pity for my travails as a single parent. I lapped up his sympathy and pity with the lust of a dog whose master offered him food and water after having left him for days without provisions. I was not above wanting Sam to be the nurturing father figure to extinguish my deprived sense of feeling "less" than others. Sam had me hook, line and sinker when he sweetened my employment pot with a munificent offer to ease my travel burdens by granting me an "unofficial," alternate schedule. The word "unofficial" was code for anything he misinterpreted as a narcissistic slight, which was then grounds for threatening to pull the plug on this "special" favor. This special favor was to be kept just between us. I never doubted his contention that the Human Resources department, was likely to strike down this arrangement as a work-rules violation. So it remained our dirty little worst-kept secret.

Everyone in the agency knew about my alternate schedule. I am not sure who, if anyone, enjoyed a similar arrangement. No one to my knowledge complained, presumably because I was well liked, worked hard, and visibly struggled to manage my life as a single parent. I did nothing to dispel the fiction that my interstate commute was much longer than any of my colleagues' intrastate commutes. Meanwhile I gratefully enjoyed my empathetic, compassionate and kind work family.

Throughout my six-year tenure Sam periodically threatened, yet never revoked, my alternate schedule. Had he done so, my commute back and forth during rush hour would have with alarming regularity totaled four hours instead of two. Sam, I remain grateful to you for not following through on your threats. You had a big heart and your flexibility permitted me to maintain a part-time private practice and meet my obligations to my children. Thank you!

By 2006, my part-time private practice had grown to the point that my evenings were now long and arduous extensions of my days. Something had to give. I could not hit the ground running at 5:00 AM, drive all over this New England state and then meet with patients until 9:30 PM. It got very old. Strapped for time, I left for work at the crack of dawn with a cooler that after a few hours contained a tepid breakfast, lunch, and dinner, none of which were designed to be eaten at a temperature fit for feeding baby food to infants.

From the time I had entered graduate school my goal had been to enter full-time private practice as a psychotherapist. For years, this goal overwhelmed me the same way my mother's expectations that I manage in her absence when she removed her hover-like attentions overwhelmed me. All neurotic reservations aside, the time fast approached in the spring of 2006 for me to take the plunge. Unfortunately, neither Dad nor Sam were figures for me to identify with "in the mettle department." Each was unlikely to surrender job security for the speculative advantages of starting their own businesses.

I was trained early on not to mirror yet be prepared to take on anxieties others wanted no part of. This was an environmental constant of my formative years, the way tropical temperatures are a constant in the Virgin Islands. Now I resonated to consistent responses old and new. I feared how the synergy between my anxieties about private practice and the anxious responses to my departure by a largely security conscious, unionized work force, might swell the tides of my apprehensions to flood-like levels like the rivers in New Jersey after Hurricane Sandy.

When I went public with my decision to leave this plum state job and forsake a future pension, my colleagues predictably registered concern the way they might if a patient with a history of suicide attempts reported suicidal ideation to them. Many looked gravely concerned as if ready to call the mobile crisis team and have me evaluated for commitment to a psychiatric hospital. I was one part scared to death to leave my cushy agency job and one part angry at myself for selling myself short.

In the winter and spring of 2006 my message to Sam was increasingly: "Put your money where your mouth is and act on your threats. If you punitively take away my early schedule, I'll do what

I have to do to take care of myself." This resulted in a host of petty games on his part meant to make my days needlessly difficult. For example, instead of leaving my satellite work station at 3:30 PM and driving straight to my private practice or picking up my kids, I had to now first return to the home office and sign out.

What came next was a vengefully sweet rewriting of an old story. Here I was, the longstanding "panties boy" going toe-to-toe in the ring with a man whom some colleagues, in addition to myself, believed took a perverse delight in reducing co-workers to tears. I earned in some quarters a reputation as heroic. I only hoped that the entire kernel of truth here was not simply that Sam was a proxy for acts of revenge against my father. If that were the crux of the case, then my leap into private practice might be a reckless endangerment of my own welfare, like falling on my own sword in taking the leap into private practice. As my aggression welled up, I acted the role of the trigger happy gunslinger and erred on the side of beating Sam to the draw. I must admit that, in spite of my grave fears that my aggression was misplaced, out of proportion to Sam's offenses and therefore embarrassingly inappropriate, I proudly forged on. I did so, silently cheered on by colleagues who saluted my bravery. Finally at 52 years of age, I for once felt more heroic than cowardly.

Unlike with Dad, Peter, Sue or a host of girlfriends, this time I was the one walking out as opposed to being walked out on. What a dignified farce was Sam's farewell pizza party for me! But the war was over and I was on that afternoon my gracious best. I had come a very long way fighting the good fight with my own baggage, from my days as a 20-something kid working as a bellman who slung other folks' Louis Vuitton luggage onto carts.

CHAPTER 9

THE WOMAN OF MY DREAMS? WELL ALMOST!

A re there such things as accidents of fate? The debate rag-es on. I choose to believe not. For arguments sake I will offer my pet theory about my first face-to-face encounter with "Gwyneth" the day after my father's funeral, which is that some vast contextual network of potential possibilities I will call "Team Universe" somehow determined this outcome on the fly from an infinite number of menu options.

I had yet to recover from my euphoric hangover after drinking in way too much praise for my stirring eulogy as I looked ahead to our first meeting. The father of my imagination bubbled glee-fully over my first class tribute as he boarded the next flight to Heaven. This was my prescription for happiness filled by "The Great Pharmacist" in the sky.

The shaky pretext under which I met Gwyneth, a soon to be licensed professional counselor, in her office, was to rent office hours. My private practice, to my repeating disbelief, now busted from the seams of another sublet. Even had this sight for sore eyes been a slum lord, I am not sure I would have applied the brakes on our handshake deal.

This beautiful will-o-the-wisp of a woman – thin, lithe, and dressed in a tasteful and dignified manner – had me salivating with carnal desire from the get go. Her long black hair was securely gathered atop her head with a tiara. To yours truly, a descendant of a bloodline that was as crude as oil extracted from some ocean basin, here strode a woman of refinement, which made her irresistible forbidden fruit to my class-conscious conscience.

Gwyneth was well proportioned. If she had any peacock in her, such demure attire was a dead giveaway she defensively stifled it. This stinger-less queen bee moved gently as if not to not startle the air molecules. Unlike Sue, who was a pads and helmet scrimmage partner, Gwyneth was one gentle soul even a rabbit or squirrel would not skittishly approach. Her gait, consistent with her attire, conveyed an air of quiet dignity, balance, and equanimity. If there was anyone that got my juices flowing, it was a beautiful, intelligent woman whose demeanor silently screamed "I am somebody." Little was I willing to consider at the time that appearances might be very deceiving. No doubt on this occasion I was every bit the equal of the finest tailors who ever practiced their craft with my custom-tailored first impression.

I think both of us implicitly knew once our eyes met that this ostensible landlord-tenant interview and professional networking opportunity was in truth a first date for coffee. She was in the midst of a divorce, and I opined on this topic that evening with the confidence of a professional waiter who committed to memory all the ingredients of every special on the menu. I offered many reasons why it was lunacy for anyone to get involved with a person in the emotional throes of separation and divorce. Who was I kidding? With the benefit of hindsight, this was me on my knees begging her to recognize that my longings to be loved were about to become a river that swelled beyond its banks and warning her to erect levees quickly or else we would both be swept away by the currents of my libido. As soon as we left the coffee shop, I took Gwyneth's hand, escorted her to her car, kissed her goodnight on the cheek, and off we went, white-water rafting without a raft.

To mindful selves who actively dial into the moment and its nuances of meaning as opposed to dialing out on some unleashed reverie, our informal agreement to be more than landlord and tenant was a very bad idea. It was about as bad an error in judgment as a physician suggesting an alcohol-based cough suppressant to a recovering alcoholic patient.

Our styles were rather disparate and yet, our aims were surprisingly similar. We ruthlessly pursued our agendas and did our absolute best to hide this fact from ourselves and therefore by extension, each other. Gwyneth did so on her tiptoes, so as not to awaken her faculties of reasoning to her unconscious aims. I did so making a racket, hoping she was as hard of hearing of my true intentions as I was. She received style points for social etiquette I sorely lacked. Yet, any way you sliced it we were both "special," as in entitled adults who could not be expected to make loving sacrifices to honor each other's needs. The rules of mutual fair play applied to those fictionalized others who had such an easier time of it than we had as children. Gwyneth wore it on her covered sleeve like some faint hint of last night's perfume, and I wore it like the scent of a man who just spent all night in a hookah lounge. My freshly-minted girlfriend was not one to see this about herself. My own grandiosity remained a potential sore point for me. I still wanted to act the part of the little boy and, as was the culture inside my natal family, not be held accountable for the consequences of my actions.

If I had not become so much wiser licking my wounds of grief after Gwyneth and I parted ways, I might have chosen to offer you an abbreviated version of this affair of the heart and fast forwarded this memoir to what I pray is my swan song of romances. But I will not do so, because just maybe you will learn something from my follies about the bewitching earmarks of your own custom-fitted Venus fly traps.

The first year of our relationship was an indulgent fantasy, exciting in its novelty in part because it was dangerous. We both foolishly ceded authority to our estranged spouses and then covertly defied their trumped up authority. Our covert defiant voices were echoed by our sex life as well. Gwyneth was uninhibited, with an appetite for sex that was as large as her appetite for food was small. For someone who grew up with the experience that his penis was possessed by others and the aim was largely to make sure that it did not grow into a symbol of autonomous power, to have a girlfriend who took great pleasure in my potent symbol of male power was just what the doctor ordered, a tonic for my self-esteem. Our relationship had a delicious rhythm. Once a week we met for an afternoon delight. We spoke daily about our lives, occasionally stole an hour together on the weekends we had our kids, and were together a good part of the weekends that we did not. For a while, this was a very workable symbiosis. We implicitly knew to not ask for anything that could lead to conflict. Consequently, we did not test the reality of our fantasies about what life might be like together. Despite the denial of reality, this relationship was by far and away the healthiest and most satisfying relationship of my life up to that point in time.

The cliff notes version of history's footprint on Gwyneth's ongoing narrative is that she grew up in an alcoholic family, where the alcoholic patriarch hushed his potential critics with the power of payouts from his purse. In his daughter's case, there were more promises of carrots than transfers of ownership. One might say Gwyneth nearly dislocated her shoulder over the years of reaching in futility for the dangled carrots. Based on what I knew about this family of origin, I should have run to the bank with the following interpretation and invested it in a certificate of deposit. Gwyneth, fresh off her divorce from husband "Carl," was eligible by legal mandate to lifetime alimony payments. Carl over the course of their two decades marriage acquitted himself well as a stand in for her Dad, a walking hurt locker of frustrated desires. In my less than humble opinion, Hell would sooner have assumed a look and feel of the last Ice Age before Gwyneth might have chosen to live with me and relinquish these cash subsidies. By law, they were to evaporate once Carl entered a motion to rescind his alimony payments, as he would have done had Gwyneth and I formalized our relationship via marriage. Translated, Gwyneth, who quietly yet triumphantly garnished Daddy's carrots each month, was not about to give them up.

In August of 2006, nearly two years into our relationship, I launched my full-time private practice. In economic terms no one in their right mind would ever have confused me with Gwyneth's Dad. Likewise, no one would have considered calling my practice a cash cow. All you had to do was visit my one-bedroom apartment and do the math based on your observation that I slept on a convertible sofa in the living room so my kids had a bedroom of their own. Carl may have lost his wife but was not anytime soon to lose the title "provider" while she and I continued to date each other. Gwyneth's two part-time jobs could not finance the charming little home she purchased for her kids during the last year of our time together.

To employ a baseball metaphor, the scouting report on me was that I struck out too much and lacked power to all economic fields. But oh how I could use my emotional intelligence to go from base to base, and I eventually stole Gwyneth's heart with the vacuum cleaner-like way I fielded all her questions about co-parenting in divorce. Even better, Gwyneth was taken by how I commanded myself from the dugout, barking protests when Carl brushed her off the plate with some "chin music" so that she might not get too comfortable swinging for the fences in divorce court.

How ironic that I provided Gwyneth with what I considered to be the ideal guidance I still sought. I could not see my own duplicities, knowing full well my family had doled out ample portions of such "arrogant wisdom" to undermine my efforts to be my own boss and keep me dutifully dependent on them. I bought into my own fiction that "learning from my mistakes in love" somehow invested me with psychic powers to read Gwyneth's cards. Way too often, I crossed the line with her. The gratuitous and arrogant self-appointed side of me shoved aside the respectful and concerned boyfriend side. I cringe even now to consider that I continued to wear my father's fedora and unconsciously victimize this nice woman with my best ignominious imitation of him.

Gwyneth and I were well suited as "psychotherapy lifers," therapists who double as patients and who, in their patient roles, understand the concepts of treatment beginnings and middles but not ends. My lifetime registration as a patient is in part an implicit demand that someone care for me for life, to make amends for those who did not adequately care for me as a child. Psychotherapy remained a means to modulate my "mommy hunger" and to spare me the anticipated shame and humiliation of being sent packing for being too much of an infantile burden on Gwyneth.

We both struggled with our guilt over the reactions of our kids to separation and divorce. Neither of us grew up in homes where there was enough love to go around, so sharing was trumped by competitive grabbing. This dynamic left us feeling guilty about asking our kids to share us. They were the only legitimate victims of two highly stressful, dysfunctional marriages. Now all four were forced to come to deal with the fallout from the realization that the parents they once believed loved each other forever had grown to hate each other and then split. Did they in the dark closets of their imaginations, where fear runs wild, dignify the possibility that they could be the next casualties in line?

I had been divorced since 2002, so by now my kids had learned to normalize shuttling back and forth between households, packing and unpacking their little suitcases like frequent business flyers. For Gwyneth's kids, it was fresh in their fragile psyches that their father had left home, and then their home was sold, stripping them of the comforts it held. The introduction of "Mommy's new boyfriend" into her son's life held the potential to be sand or sugar in the gas tank of our romantic vehicle. We were quietly relieved to put off the inevitable introductions.

Meanwhile, we did our best to attend to our kids. It was much easier to focus on kids' needs than to focus on our "adult" needs, which begged the question how competent we were to manage our own lives after divorce. We continued to nurture an attachment with each other without giving much thought to us blending our families together.

Once Gwyneth found her sea legs after her divorce was finalized, our honeymoon was officially over. This predictable development was credit to her resilience and cause for her boyfriend to say: "Good job, Gwyneth!" I was frankly ambivalent about her positive adjustment to her single parent status. Had I bought that Gwyneth chose to love me, as opposed to convincing herself she loved me for fear of her prospects without me, such a turn of events would have been unprecedented for me. I did not know what it meant to be securely attached from codependent, the way some people do not know what it is like to be comfortably alone with themselves without being unconscious, as in asleep or semi-conscious with a drink in their hands.

I readily confused her with my mother. I found myself angry, put upon, and disappointed in Gwyneth for being Gwyneth. She was rather conflict-avoidant in her dealings with opportunistic merchants who were not above using her weakness to their advantage. At this juncture her business dealings were none of my business. Yet, my mind linked such episodes to events early in life, when my conflict-avoidant mother did not stand up for me when I required her protection. Gwyneth had now become someone for me who could not take adequate care of herself and by extension would not serve my interests as well. I felt obligated to coach her aggressively, and I slowly but surely pushed her away. I blamed her unfairly for my own hitting of the "play" button on some old recordings. At this time in my life, I was convinced that those who commanded respect, unlike my parents, adopted a policy of zero tolerance for perceived slights. Unfortunately, this was a primitive and thoughtless reaction to my former passivity in the face of aggression. "Loss" eventually schooled me in the virtues of diplomacy. For now, I was fresh off fights with my work supervisor and was convinced that the only way I would ever get respect in this world was to make sure that no one, including Gwyneth, got the wrong idea about me being a pushover.

To be bluntly honest with you my confessor, to get hot under the collar at my lover, this survivor of developmental trauma was insensitive bordering on cruel. When I was cruel, Gwyneth would flinch as if being whipped but would barely protest, leaving me feeling like my sadistic father. I hated both of us for Gwyneth mirroring me this way. I began to push her away with my anger as a cover for my fears that she would see how identified I was with the childlike images of myself and leave me. It certainly did not help matters that stress in our relationship made it increasingly difficult for Gwyneth to achieve orgasm in the bedroom. When she introduced a super-charged dildo I nicknamed "Moby" to our lovemaking, I felt once again like an Oedipal loser, and immediately assumed she intended to humiliate me for failing her. This supposition was my rationalization for tapping into a reservoir of historical rage out of proportion with any provocation on Gwyneth's part.

The day I met her son "Cliff" in late 2007 was the day it dawned on me that our relationship was in trouble. There was no way for us to cross paths during his early adolescence and co-exist under the same roof.

Cliff was raised by a sweet and fragile mother. All indications were that with Carl's exit from Gwyneth's life, Cliff now auditioned as his mother's protector, and I was his main competition for the job. As a child whose reality testing was a work in progress, he needlessly, yet understandably, feared that if Mom could force Dad to look for family employment elsewhere, he might be the next casualty of his mother's downsized life. He held a gun to Gwyneth's head by threatening to go live with his Dad if he did not get his way with her. Such threats left Gwyneth that much more reticent than she already was to rein in her little tyrant.

Cliff began a regimen of pushups to strengthen his arms and chest. Gwyneth found it endearingly sweet that her son wished to be her protector. Frankly, as embarrassed as I am to admit this, I felt menaced by him. Fact or fiction, his muscle-flexing conditioning program had me conceiving him to be a nation-state mobilizing its armaments to wage war against me. One war stratagem was his choosing video games to play with me that I knew nothing about and of which he had achieved a measure of mastery. He delighted at dancing on the grave of my incompetence as if he had read the scouting report on how my father had treated me. It was an important yardstick of my growth that I found a way to respectfully and firmly ask Cliff to treat me with respect and consideration if he had any interest in me as a playing partner. Gwyneth and I were very attached at this stage so she persisted with her own wish that her tacit refusal to set limits on Cliff's behavior would not interfere with the two families spending time together. I persisted with my own wish that Gwyneth would eventually rein Cliff in because she loved me.

Paired with my fears was sorrow at watching Cliff flounder. He struck me as desperately needing and not finding the guidance and structure required for him to focus on learning the prosocial ethics of success. If there was anything I learned watching one man-child after another cycle in and out of New England prisons, it was that the mix of parental abdications and abuses of authority inside families sowed the seeds of antisocial behavior. Cliff, as far as I know, has not lived up to my delinquent predictions for him.

I thanked God that my kids were girls. I knew it was in me to potentially disgrace myself if a son openly defied me, by subjecting a son to the humiliation inflicted on me by my father and to a lesser degree by my brother. Here I was about to relive multiple childhood nightmares in the process of trying to forge a relationship with a kid whose inflated ego left him a giant porcupine. My best guess is that he intuitively hoped that mocking me would either send me packing or incite me to acts of cruel revenge that would make his mother never talk to me again. To my self-satisfaction, I did neither.

I felt bad for him and was quite sad that more was not expected of him, which I believe left him fearing he was not capable of much and not worth expecting more of. Both parents failed to ensure their son did his homework and turn it in on time. There was no doubt in my mind that Cliff's parents saw my encouragements of them to exercise benevolent authority over their son as me trying to subjugate his free will. They all gave authority a bad name and therefore resisted me.

For a while I brought my kids around, and I will admit that Cliff did not openly taunt me or goad me into power struggles while they were present. He liked my daughters and did not risk me getting pissed off and not bringing them with me. It bothered me much more than it bothered them when Cliff did not play fairly with them. They were amused. I was annoyed. Gwyneth unsurprisingly behaved in a manner I imagine not dissimilar to how she behaved as a child when her father made a drunken fool of himself. She acted as if it was not happening.

The issue came to a head one Christmas when Cliff did not thank me for his gifts. It was the final straw in a long line of what I interpreted to be intentional slights, and I had finally had enough. In private I let Gwyneth know that until the time came that she forbade such disrespect, my kids were not coming around. I certainly could have been more compassionate and more empathetic to Gwyneth, as she came by her character weaknesses honestly. I am embarrassed to admit that in retrospect I recognize that my need for her to demonstrate more respect for me had to do in part with my own lack of self-respect.

Back in 2008, I was still looking outside myself for appreciation and validation, when the problem actually was that I did not sufficiently give myself credit for what I had achieved. It was imperative that I took charge of myself and see my worries for what they were – vestiges of a telescopic parental lens that were fixated on me in order to defend against their own archaic poorly understood worries about their safety and security, worries which had shaped their helicopter-like watchfulness over me. I did not have much of a say back then over the castrating impact of their traumatized brains on my self-esteem. Potentially I did now. I also, as you already know, confused kind forbearance with weakness, and so I felt compelled to draw a line in the sand and express zero tolerance for Gwyneth's indulgence of her son's adolescent jabs.

In all fairness to Gwyneth and Cliff, had I been ready to be the traditional head of any two-parent household, I would have assertively taken Cliff under my wing and found a way to cultivate an alliance with him. The kid had no one he could depend on to take charge of his life in a benevolently authoritative manner. So he learned that he had to take matters into his own hands and do his best to control the actions of those he needed to survive. There was no reason why he could not retain the love of his father and have my love. We had different strengths and he might have been a whole lot better off learning from both of us. There was also no reason why his mother could not have my love and Cliff's at the same time.

The challenge Cliff presented coincided with another major challenge, namely adapting to my new role as business owner. This hat would leave me chronically worried about myself for the next few years in ways not dissimilar to how my parents worried about me. My parents catastrophized normal growing pains as if they feared I would not adapt to new developmental challenges. Now it was my turn. Back then I was still haunted by performance anxieties and crises of confidence if patients chose to not continue in my care. Mediocre performance was acceptable inside a New England mental health agency. This was not the case for the upper-middle class people paying me their hard earned money; they expected much more in return than the indigent wards of the state who had no choice but to accept uneven standards of care by those assigned as their advocates.

I did a less-than stellar job accepting my growing pains as a first-time business owner. When anxious and overwhelmed, I often misguidedly summoned the image of a mother whose enveloping pity only made matters worse. (Dad was seldom if ever comforting.) Her idea of being a good mother was to worry about me when there was nothing to worry about. So I walked around either worried about myself or, as was my preference, worried about someone else. That someone else was often Gwyneth.

We still enjoyed moments when we could leave our worldly problems behind and enjoy each other's company. However, those moments became less frequent as the frictions attendant to disparate parenting styles intruded on our fantasized love affair. Arrogant perfectionism became a defense against my confusion and self-doubts over making a mess of my own life and those of my kids. I looked to Gwyneth to validate perspectives and reassure me that I was competent, all the while blind to how much I fueled her passive-aggressive defiance and opposition of me by my obnoxious disrespect of her. Wishes aside, she was part of a greater universe reminding me it was dancing to many tunes besides mine alone, and that the more I resisted this idea, the less cooperation it offered in meeting my needs.

Gwyneth had long since stopped idealizing me. Early in my tenure in private practice, I found this idealization from my patients. Even if I could not fix them, I was relaxed and confident basking in the glow of their aggrandized regard for me. Of course, paradoxically, my insecurities were the architects of my own rejection, as I too often cultivated an unhealthy dependency at my patients' expense. When they figured out consciously or unconsciously that they had "been had," such ruptures were not easily repaired. I am very much up front these days with patients about what I can do and what I cannot do for them.

In Gwyneth's dealings with her son, I increasingly confused her with my mother who had been so weak and impotent in her dealings with all members of our family. I had spent thousands of dollars and decades trying to come to terms with a mother who turned me into a spoiled and grandiose child while neglecting a host of needs that left me ill-prepared to manage my own affairs.

Gwyneth began to feel burdensome to me, not unlike my mother. To worry about her in a disrespectful and inconsiderate manner left me feeling burdened by her needs, insecure about committing myself to her, and left her doubting her own reasoning and judgment. She was under fire as I increasingly lost my ability to see her being her as anything but attacking my self-importance.

Despite all my years working as a bellman and all my years as a psychoanalytic patient and practitioner, I could not effectively manage my baggage.

Gwyneth never once told me she was more and more dubious about our long-term prospects. But how could this not be the case with yours truly fueling her humiliated outrage? She hung around, accepted the support she had learned to depend on, satisfied the needs she could, and did her best to accommodate to the rest. When in her presence, I hid my shameful concerns about myself and rationalized that she would not be any more helpful than my parents. I preferred to either focus on her struggles or pretend for a while that none of this stuff existed. When I needed to attend to my own business, or began to worry about taking care of my own business, I retreated to my apartment so I could unselfconsciously engage in what were superstitious rituals of worrying about the future, as if such worries would magically shield me from the fruition of my worst fears.

I loved this sweet woman as best as I could love anyone but by 2008, most of that love was eclipsed by hate and rage. Gwyneth got the message loud and clear. I was clearly not the guy I portrayed myself to be during the honeymoon phase of our relationship when I expected much less of her and gave her much more. Soon Gwyneth expressed prophetic fears I would leave her. My efforts to reassure her rang hollow for both of us. My false comfort was probably my way of saying that I was not prepared to deal with my own separation anxieties, so I did my best to placate hers. But I could see the handwriting on the wall.

I increasingly behaved more like a better-educated version of my impatient, intolerant, father with his wicked anger management issue. Gwyneth mirrored me as a persecutor and froze as if under my abusive dominion. This only heightened my sadistic tendencies. Nothing got my blood to boil like a woman who reminded me of my masochistic mother who liked to cry foul while denying responsibility for her cunning and deceitful manipulative ways. Gwyneth was neither cunning nor deceitful but she was quite the masochist nonetheless. Here I was so attached to this sweet and beautiful woman, and yet I knew in my heart this relationship was a dead end. Gwyneth, true to her nature, would quit and stay and wait for me to pull the trigger.

One Friday night in March of 2008, after a particularly mean-spirited display on my part before and during a high school performance by my daughter's theater group, Gwyneth asked me again when the kids could get together. I had told her countless times that they would never get together until she assured me that if Cliff behaved in a disrespectful manner, she would intervene. The fight escalated and continued at her place, culminating in my screaming at her on the way out the door.

I was never to return except for the following Saturday when I dropped off all of her possessions left in my apartment, by the front door of her home. We had one very tearful phone conversation that was in essence a post mortem for our three and a half year relationship, during which I requested and was denied another opportunity to work things out. With my anger and rage having lifted like the morning mist, I was now mourning more losses than I had ever bargained for. Gwyneth wrote me a very gracious and strikingly unemotional letter, during which she thanked me for the best three and a half years of her life. That was the end.

For the next five or six weeks I pined for Gwyneth, and apparently for the mother of every stage of my development, the one I missed and the one I always wished for but could not have. I am certain that I was also mourning a multitude of failed strategies to garner love. I did not need a mother figure anymore. I had to muster more respect for this reengineered self that could now soothe, regulate, satisfy, nurture, and discipline on its own.

You could say I was the analyzed equivalent of the handy, dandy machine that dices, purées, juliennes, chops, and shreds. I was angry as hell for not having taken myself more seriously. Yes, I recognize how much this must sound like a broken record. This time around, instead of beating myself up over having wound up at one more dead end, I was hell bent to secure my treasure: a secure and healthy marriage partner. It was time to declare myself fit to take charge of that frightened, insecure, self-doubting little boy inside of me and deal with him for what he was; recollections of ways of being that were once adaptive and now had to be relegated to the sidelines where he could indulge in imaginative play and not get me in trouble.

Here I was, now 54-years old, being called for another false start. However you slice it, whatever reordering had taken place, I had not yet taken the leap of faith and corrected the flaws in my intuitive expectations. I still acted according to scripts written long in the past. Now without Gwyneth, I had no choice but to re-claim parts of myself I had conveniently disowned, disavowed, and pushed on her to suffer for me. These were shameful and guilt-ridden parts that saw me spinning my damaged rudder and going around in circles like a toy boat in a bathtub.

In my practice, I cried before I saw my first patient of the day, between patients if I had a break, and at the end of the day. My psychoanalyst at the time, Dr. L, offered me a priceless sugges-tion when she said, "Check your grief outside the door of your of-fice before your next patient arrives." This compartmentalization worked. I did not burst out into tears during sessions and lapse into blabbering hysteria and apologize for being useless to them because I missed my girlfriend. I did my job. Was I at my best? No way, José! I was very far from my best. Did my patients notice something was bothering me? I am sure they did, though no one complained.

I feared that without Gwyneth I would be as incompetent as I had been without my mother in my 20s: helpless and hopeless. As chaotic as my internal world felt as I went through this period of adaptive reorganization that required me to find new attachments for these unbound, chaotic energies, I managed to hold it together with the assistance of my friends and my shrink.

Dr. L was very patient with me, even as I tried to blame her for not having woken me up earlier so that "reason" might have prevailed and I might have ended this relationship years before I had so much invested in it. The turning point in my mourning process was Dr. L asking me if I thought I needed medication as a temporary adjunctive treatment until the tides of emotion receded or just dried out. This was a very effective tactical intervention on her part. Dr. L joined my resistance to moving on by saying in essence, "Maybe you are worse off than I had previously contemplated and you need pharmaceutical assistance to soothe yourself so that you can restore your perspective on this state of affairs." These were fighting words! I took this as a personal affront to my analyzed manhood. This paradoxical intervention was designed to get me to reflect and understand that perhaps I was playing an unconscious "victim card," similar to the strategy my mother often employed to punish others for not rescuing her from herself. Dr. L was helping me test my fallacious reality by saying in essence, "I can't save you from the consequences of you letting yourself drown in your own tears, so please give some thought to what your aims are here."

Like magic, the floodgates of tears were reduced to an occasional drizzle. I had turned the corner. Again, I was too slow and too late to recognize that old autopilots were flying me where autonomous reasoning dictated I dare not go. I was finally where I needed to be; sick and tired of being sick and tired. Justice would only be served by me recognizing the many sides of me as collectively good enough to move forward with a proactive, disciplined and determined approach to create my own trail maps. It had been seven weeks since I had shamelessly stormed out of Gwyneth's home. I felt as if I had gone through the equivalent of seven weeks of "cold turkey" from heroin addiction. I felt horrible much of this period and yet the "I" required for me to help patients and manage my affairs stayed online most of the time.

If I could cope with this loss and keep moving forward then it was time to channel the same grit and determination toward chasing my dreams. Dr. L had said in a variety of ways that as I progressed through my journey and developed my emotional muscles I would be capable of performing more work, more efficiently. I now recognized that rewriting my narratives had to be a daily exercise of intentional will to combat my ingrained tendencies. I would have to learn to do whatever it took to find true love or whatever else was on my bucket list. My wishful thinking had deceived me for decades and now it was time to stop letting it thwart me. There was nothing inherently defective about me. These flaws could be accounted for and corrected.

Top athletes and top business people trained daily for success and were hard workers. The big question on my mind was whether I could be passionately engaged without being distracted by the yet-to-materialize final outcome. Would the end justify the means? Could I enjoy the day-to-day process irrespective of where I wound up? I was not sure, but I thought that if I kept moving in a disciplined manner, I would wind up in more accomplished places. When push came to shove I found great comfort in recognizing that I was always doing the best I could do with my internal resources and external supports. Furthermore, I was exactly where I was comfortable being and when I was ready to move to another space I would. I had to develop my faith in opening myself to the wisdom of the moment.

As it turned out, success in full-time private practice required that I learn to relax and immerse myself in the moment and trust that such mindful immersion "in being" with my patients would guarantee a living far greater than my current standard of living. There were many factors that affected the durability of a patient's attachment to me. In fact, I found that my empathic failures were indispensable to my patient's movements toward self-sufficiency mediated by their positive adaptations to new and stressful challenges, or what Heinz Kohut termed "optimal frustration." We must all learn to cope with minor insults and injuries, and find ways to repair relational rifts in the service of building more flexible and resilient ties to others. Sometimes I screwed up big time and patients not only stayed but we grew closer as a result of such a crisis in the relationship. Sometimes what I would have anticipated to be a minor slight was not forgiven and the aggrieved party walked right out the door. Sometimes they did so without as much as a goodbye after being in my practice for years. Such losses were painful to mourn. There were other times patients disappeared without as much as a peep, and I was left scratching my head. If I were to make a go of my practice, I had to learn to practice as if I were independently wealthy no matter how financially challenged I was. My gift to them was to be an attachment figure of respect and not resist their efforts to fly the therapeutic coop and leave guilt-free, so they could own and integrate the gifts of my being with them to enhance their internal navigational systems. If they left prematurely by either of our estimations, there was no way in Hell they would ever return for additional flying lessons if they suspected that my overriding interest was to rent them time and space in my hangar. What was counterintuitive for me, and yet so gratifying, was to see the relief on the faces of my patients when I celebrated their rights of self-determination and offered them on the way out a corrective experience of parental figures who, for a variety of self-serving interests, had tried to clip their wings.

If truth be told, much of my success in private practice has been due to the influence of high-intensity interval training, which cultivated a highly disciplined, highly energetic, and mindful work ethic. I may not be the most talented clinician, but across the board, from building an internet presence and marketing my practice, to a relentlessly passionate interest in learning what it means to be fully present in the room with another human being, I have out-worked, and by extension have in many cases out-performed, many of my peers. Now, so much the stronger and wiser for having processed experiences in the spheres of work and love, I declared my readiness for an enduring partnership.

CHAPTER 10

"SCHNITZELVILLE," WHERE LIFE IS GOOD AS GOOD CAN BE

This chapter is the final stretch of an ultramarathon that with every step forward brought me back in time to recollections of parents impatient and incredulous that I would waste my time and theirs inviting them to tour my laboratory of grand plans for my future. Let's call this back and forth the mourning of all that I wished my parents to be and were not, which subsequently paved the way for my ascension to the throne of my life. This notion of "person as creator" was so foreign to them and their disdain for such frivolous wastes of time, once so unnerving and injurious to my fledgling self-esteem that early on I closed up shop, convinced that such virtual play was a sign of immaturity they impatiently commanded me to outgrow. Each time my mind returned in time, trying in vain to create some coherence to a narrative where there was little, I would for a while default to the once idealized perspectives of my parents and be seized by shameful thoughts like: *Who are you kidding, passing yourself off as a serious artist? Will you grow up already and stop being so childishly self-indulgent?* So forgive me if from time to time I wave my arms in triumph and pump my fists in exuberant celebration. I will be the first to tell you that I am very short on physical courage. Nevertheless, I am very proud that time and again, bout after anxious bout, I went against the grain of everything I was taught to believe about myself to demonstrate a profile in courage worthy of a purple heart by my standards if no one else's.

By the beginning of May 2008, the spigot of my grief over the loss of Gwyneth had been open for two months and my tears, once the flow of an open fire hydrant, slowed to an occasional trickle. It dawned on me that if I chose to let my unconscious narratives operate without oversight, then my search for love would forever remain "Mission Impossible." My laser-like focus at this juncture was to learn from my mistakes with Gwyneth. I quickly clarified and translated my values for a successful partnership to an unambiguous and frank online portrait of who I was, what I was looking for in a mate, and what a potentially interested party would find in me as a partner. I bought a subscription to J-Date and subjected all who crossed paths with me to the bluntest prosecutorial scrutiny imaginable. I pitied anyone who thought they could play games with me and waste my time. After partnering with Sue, and later Gwyneth, I was on a mission and channeled anger at myself for returning to my "wishing well" over and over again toward the task at hand. Just because I was not screaming like my salty-tongued father did not mean that the next object of my desires would find me any less intimidating and offensive. We spoke by phone that first time, and thankfully she did not. Laura, please accept my apologies for my bull-headed, empathy-light test of your fitness to stay the course of my slow but steady maturation.

Like Glinda the Good Witch beckoning the Munchkins out of hiding after Dorothy's house fell on and killed the Wicked Witch of the East, my shrinks were beckoning my autonomous mind to not be afraid to emerge and overcome my inhibitions to sing and dance to my own beat. This was easier said than done, as there were way too many times I felt all alone and frightened, swallowed up by

the disorienting fears that seized Dorothy and her group of min-
strels walking through domains controlled by the Wicked Witch
of the West. I had not had a secure attachment figure outside the
treatment rooms since long-expired friendships that predated the
era of my marriage to Sue. Once Sue and I separated, I reverted
to an island-like, avoidant attachment style outside the treatment
room. My ambition was to prove I could survive a heaping plate of
adult responsibilities all by my lonesome as I still clung to the men-
tality of a rescue dog who expected to be abused and abandoned if
he got too close for comfort. You might say that I could not muster
sufficient faith in my innate intelligence to deliver the baby that
was my mindful creative self into the world without the assistance
of a midwife. Little did I know she was on her way.

It was only a few weeks on J-Date before I found myself gaz-
ing upon the picture of a bewitching stunner. In her profile, she
wrote about her loyalty to others and how she worked hard to nurture those attachments she valued. In a world where the Internet
produced successive generations of stimulation junkies with sub-
clinical attention deficits, here was a 21st century woman who in
many respects belonged to a previous generation. Her name was
Laura.

She was (and still is) a head turner, and I expected that she
would treat me like a concert promoter asking fans to camp out
overnight for the chance to win a lottery drawing for a ticket. Yes,
I was prepared for the possibility that a first date would feel like a
hurried audition. I had that experience on more than one occasion. Online dating is a cyberworld for some who prefer to pass
off last year's Halloween costume as their authentic identities. For
those who are bottomless pits of early unacknowledged needs, to-
morrow's invitation to flirt forever holds the promise to perform
compensatory magic in a manner yesterday's flesh and blood pros-
pect could not. It is easy to preserve such fantasies when, over
time, there is an endless stream of Prince Charmings ready to

audition for the part. So here I was, standing outside Laura's apartment building on a gloriously warm and sunny early evening of May 31, 2008. Her building and surrounding courtyard were situated in Washington Heights, Manhattan, an odd mix of yuppies, Bohemian Greenwich village types, soon to expire German Jews of the Holocaust Era, and Serbian tradespeople. Punctual to a fault, I was 15 minutes early, which gave me time to take the following inventory on what I had to offer this woman. I was fit and attractively dressed. That made for two checks in the plus column. In the minus column were check marks next to my looks that had gone the way of my hair years earlier. Then there was a check mark next to socioeconomic status as well. I barely earned enough income to manage my expenses living in a one-bedroom apartment. My bedroom was my living room, as the kids occupied bunk beds in the lone bedroom. Oh yes, how about those two "developing liabilities," one anchored in adolescence and the other on the cusp? Finally, my ex-wife Sue stood at the periphery of my life more than ready to disabuse anyone of the notion that I deserved a ranking any higher on the food chain than that of a parasite. You get the gist of how self-conscious I was about my emotional baggage. How could I be anything but an also-ran in this race for Laura's hand? Would she even remember my name three weeks from now?

So here I was, done with my inventory. Now, while I paced just outside Laura's courtyard, I was not aware of two very important facts that in combination might have ended any chances with this woman before we even got our feet wet. The first was that I paced back and forth like an expectant father, unaware that my lips moved while I had this rather audible conversation with myself. At least the neighbors did not call the police. The second was that Laura watched me from her living room window as I was lost in my dissociated state, oblivious to my surroundings. Lucky me, her living room window just happened to face the courtyard so she was treated to a balcony view of my entire monologue. Eventually

Laura came outside, made her presence known, and with a big gracious smile pointed to her bay window from which she had spied me and told me that she figured the guy speaking to himself was her date. One cannot account for the clout of unconscious forces of attraction. Somehow Laura found this idiosyncrasy endearing, and I felt comfortable enough to share with her that I was bracing myself for her to reject me. Well Laura, who had eyeballed my website and spoken with me by phone, had at least surmised that I was able keep the voices in my head in check long enough to create a professional presence on the Internet, did what was even more unimaginable. What happened next was an incalculable quantum leap of faith on her part that love would cure my apparent psychosis. She invited me up to her apartment and was so ebullient and comfortable as to jump in my lap and sit there for a good half hour before we even went out to dinner. Laura will tell you she was more restrained than my memory serves me, and that her lap jumping took place after dinner. I will not argue this one. Happy wife, happy life.

I am unsure how to account for our meeting on J-Date. First off, no one would ever confuse either of us with devout Jews of even the reformed kind. In fact, even though my upbringing was stamped with Jewish commandments like "thou shalt never be caught dead empty handed without a box of German coffee cake, Viennese strudel, or apple pie when visiting friends or family," neither of us were raised by devout Jews of any denomination. Laura was raised by a Scotch-English-Irish, non-practicing Protestant mother with a permanent leash on her husband, who did not dare insinuate Judaic religious rituals into their home. As a kid I was forbidden from playing ball on Yom Kippur or Rosh Hashanah. Yet outside of an invitation to a Bar Mitzvah or wedding, we never stepped inside of a synagogue to worship with other members of our tribe. My father will tell you that he could not afford a synagogue membership. However, it was the same financial falsehood and flimsy justification for him to deny me a carpet for my room or a stereo phonograph. I love you Dad, but let's face it: I come by my sometime stinginess with money honestly. There are synagogues where you can worship without officially becoming members. Bet you did not care to know that Dad!

My best guess is that Laura's registration on J-Date was a conscious desire to reconnect with the Judaic roots of her father (who, in aligning with her sister against her mother, gave Laura less attention than she deserved and needed). Murray Lander tragically died of a heart attack when Laura was only seventeen. Maybe, there were just enough similarities here for Laura to enjoy the illusion of making up for lost time with Dad. You might say that, like eating strudel and drinking coffee, dating a woman familiar with and having some affinity for the culture of my youth was likewise comforting.

Beyond having Jewish fathers in common, Laura and I could not have come to the relationship from more disparate perspectives on hunting for mates. I kid you not, Laura believed that all the good men were divorced fathers living in New Jersey. I believed that all the divorced fathers living in New Jersey came with enough emotional baggage to give Olympic weightlifters hernias. I was certain that this never-married, urbane, beautiful Manhattanite would never let me rent any space in her head to store my crap. When I met Laura, she was administrative manager of the Neue Galerie, a museum on Fifth Avenue and an aristocratic hub of fine German and Austrian art. Its benefactor, Ronald Lauder, lived in a world as far removed from my working class roots as Laura's world was distant from my life as a single parent.

Now my psychoanalytic/quantum mechanics/Buddhist philosophy tends to believe that the forces of attraction in this universe are no accident of fate. If I am wrong and this union was a chance encounter, then the best that can be said is that I made my own luck by trolling in cyberspace with my dating profile. As the lottery ads proclaim: "You can't win it if you are not in it."

On May 27, 2009, Laura and I were married in a civil ceremony by a former running buddy of mine, then the deputy mayor of our town.

What was truly remarkable was how much Laura gave up for love. I gave up very little and wound up with a King's ransom of riches. Laura on the other hand walked away from a life that had enriched her for decades. Laura was fluent in German, had worked for German organizations and had lived in Germany funded by a Fulbright Scholarship after she graduated from Ohio State University in 1982. At the time of our acquaintance, she was installed in a German expatriate community the way vintage classroom chairs and desks were once bolted to the floor. This was nonetheless a very hypocritical community that demanded undying loyalty but where people had one foot in their motherland ready to say goodbye if a good job came along, an old flame beckoned like a siren's call, or an aged parent needed assistance. They were somewhat rootless and Laura, the "hostess with the mostess," was their anchor, hosting dinner parties, and even hair-cutting parties. Meanwhile she was on call to meet their emotional needs, as well as accompany them to German-American events hosted by industry and other ex-pat friends. With both parents deceased and a sibling living in Colorado, they were her extended family.

If you subscribe to the idea that people make their own beds and therefore their own luck, then Laura wound up making her friends' rejections a self-fulfilling prophecy. They did not look kindly upon me stealing their beloved Laura from their clutches. When the group figured out that our marriage was a bit more consensual than an adult kidnapping, their envy, rage and wounded grandiosity did not permit for anything but an irreparable split.

After decades living in Manhattan embedded in an extended family of choice, Laura had now uprooted herself and moved to suburban New Jersey where loneliness took root for several years. To her credit, and to my undying gratitude, my wife, whom I fondly nicknamed Schnitzel after the popular German entrée, never complained or blamed me for the fallout from this life decision. The good news is that seven years into our marriage, Laura, in addition to being happy with me (hard for me to believe), has been richly rewarded by her industry in cultivating new friendships. She initiated a German-speakers Meetup.com group that has spawned new friendships. In addition, together we have established roots in a neighboring town's Unitarian-Universalist congregation, where from time to time I can be found singing my heart out.

Our marriage is a good news/bad news scenario like all others, and it is under such real life circumstances, as good as good can be. We are the products of two high-conflict, unhappy marriages. My wife's middle of the night raids on the refrigerator and her sleeping habits are the extent of my complaints. I have come light years in accepting what I cannot change in part due to the fact that I can now more often than not keep my wife and my mother of yore separate in my head.

Even in her nickname, I came to equate Laura with a lost comfort and safety I had not known since my early childhood. "Schnitzelville" is a place that occupied an insatiable longing in my heart for decades. Baby Boomers such as myself can picture it as a slice of Mayberry, NC, where Andy Griffith raised his television son Opie, the once childhood actor and now brilliant director, Ron Howard. It is my haven of tranquility and serenity, if not a refuge of unfaltering reasonableness like the home where Jerry Mathers of "Leave It to Beaver" fame was raised. "Schnitzelville" is a code word for a destination nearly forgotten, a delicious time in my life when I felt safe to lose myself for hours making a model airplane, playing with my plastic soldiers in a simulation of some epic Revolutionary War battle, or playing a marathon edition of the sensational Milton Bradley board game, "Life." It is a secure and safe space for me to be, where I am recognized, respected and taken seriously as a powerful architect of my own life. It is a launching pad for this rocket man to propel his individual dreams forward. Countless times I have said to my stable of shrinks that before age 10, I could remember pockets of happy days. Then happiness took a hiatus... that is until "Schnitzel" entered my life. My heart and soul literally sing tributes to her for being instrumental in creating an environment optimal for me to rewire my brain. The results have been nothing short of miraculous over the eight-year period we have been together.

She has changed everything. Like a steady voice in the air traffic control tower, when the wind and rain of emotional turbulence unsettles me, Laura helps me keep my cool. She became an extension of my psychotherapists' arms, which had been holding me together. After her arrival, I reached a tipping point in my capacities to pull lessons from the past and creatively apply them to the moment-to-moment tasks at hand.

For example, since my wife's arrival on the scene in the middle of 2008, the following developments have taken place: First, my psychotherapy practice doubled in revenues. Second, I resumed my psychoanalytic training, completed a written final case presentation that took a year to write and graduated as a psychoanalyst in 2012. Third, two-thirds of this book was written in a little bit more time than the first third was written. And lastly, in 2013 I began voice lessons and in 2016, I formed and registered a new business titled "Fountain of Youthful Music, LLC." I write and perform songs that chronicle the stories of those whose good behavior and bad inspired others to fight the good fight and rewrite their personal narratives. You might say that Fountain of Youthful Music has in part been a gratifying vehicle for me to share the magic that comes out of the examined life. What makes these musical performances so meaningful is that I can showcase the wisdom that has passed through me and others in a universal language that touches the hearts and souls of so many who might never consider formal treatment. It does not get much better for me than to have the opportunity to share my emotional intelligence and perhaps in the process inspire others to raise their own emotional IQ. Everything good that has happened to me has come from this growth process.

Laura is one of the warmest, most engaging, and accepting people I have ever met. I know what I am about to say may sound hackneyed but it is true. Laura leaves you feeling as if you are one of the most interesting people on the planet, worthy of a Barbara Walters interview. She is the antithesis of the cellphone addict who needs to check Facebook at least every 15 minutes to make sure that she is not missing out on the latest developments in the reality television shows of her closest 100 friends. With Laura, when she is in conversation with you it is as if you are the sole focus of her life, and she is delighted to spend as much time as you have exchanging information.

She is also the perfect complement to my shrink. Laura is not unflappable as in numb to the vagaries and vicissitudes of life. Not in the least. She is however, steadfastly unfailing as a barometer when the barometric pressure in the room drops because I am in a neurotic funk. Like my younger daughter Allison, my wife lets me know in no uncertain terms when I am behaving like an asshole hijacked by archaic fears I am not containing very well. She is meanwhile, wonderful in allowing me to stumble into disrespectful territory and blow off steam without getting caught up in my wind tunnels of hot air. In being like a reed in the wind that bends and does not break, Laura allows me to get a grip on my hypercharged psyche and realize that this home and this woman is not the home I grew up in, and that I am not the little boy anymore that I once was and behaved like just a moment before.

There may be nothing in this universe more valuable than having trusted others to help me reality-test confusion between the recalled identities of attachment figures in my head, and those people currently in my midst. Laura is the perfect counterpoint to my hysterical mother, making it infinitely easier for me to tease out one from the other in my head when their identities become temporarily confused. No two women could look and sound less alike, except when Laura unknowingly does her best impression of how her mother Irene related to her and offers unsolicited help to accomplish a task a two-year old could do in his sleep. How could anyone in his or her right mind confuse this petite wife of mine with my obese mother? I literally worried about my mother's heart exploding as it worked overtime to meet the energy requirements of her fat cells. It did one night in her 87th year after awaking with back pain while resident in a nursing home. But by that time I had longed stopped worrying about my mother's demise. Laura stands a little under 5'2" and never weighs more than 111 pounds. At least that's what she tells me.

Laura intuitively "gets" that her schizoid artist of a husband needs to retreat into his creative lair and be alone to lose himself in what I would describe as séance-like communions with all who have come before and all yet to arrive. Whereas my parents and Sue worried incessantly about losing control of me as I was their dedicated recycling bin for what they disowned and disavowed about themselves, Laura is a very independent person who, when I am otherwise engaged, is quite content to sit in our sunroom with her binoculars waiting for birds to drop by on our patio for a visit. If there is anything I celebrate about our union, it is the fact that my personal space is not intruded upon. I do not risk being rejected, abandoned or accused of being selfish and unloving in honoring my needs "to be." This gift of being able to relax my vigilance over guarding my personal space has permitted me to comfortably engage in intimate conversations with my wife and myself. The resulting regulated environment has helped me grow my capacity to make sense of the world and maybe more importantly hold my perspectives and the perspectives of others without fearing the onset of what I can fittingly describe as being ambushed by enemy fire. Some say the highest compliment you can pay a player on any team is that he or she makes others better players. This is my wife's claim to fame.

Growing up, if anyone took me seriously it was an idealized, over-the-top taking seriously. My parents loved to brag to their friends about how much more wonderful I was than I really was. Laura does not gush about my creative endeavors but mirrors them with the respect they deserve. I have no idea what the future holds for me as a writer of books or singer of songs. But Laura validates exactly what I know to be true, and that is that my artistic endeavors are worth investing in. My wife did not blink an eye over me investing to publish this book sight unseen, and is behind me full throttle with my singer-songwriting vehicle, Fountain of Youthful Music. Of course, we are not missing any mortgage payments to finance my projects. Everybody needs somebody sometime to hold and pump oxygen into his or her dreams of possibilities. With Laura, I am all set to chase them.

EPILOGUE

"You do not need to leave your room. Remain
sitting at your table and listen. Do not even listen,
simply wait, be quiet still and solitary. The world
will freely offer itself to you to be unmasked, it has
no choice, it will roll in ecstasy at your feet."
"By believing passionately in something that still
does not exist, we create it. The nonexistent is
whatever we have not sufficiently desired."

– Franz Kafka

AUTHOR BIOGRAPHY

Mitchell Milch, LCSW, is a licensed clinical social worker who practices psychotherapy as a sole practitioner. Milch earned a master's degree in social work in 1992 from Yeshiva University—the Wurzweiler School of Social Work. He completed a six-year certificate in psychoanalysis through the Center for Psychoanalysis and Psychotherapy of New Jersey in 2012.

A longtime runner, Milch first began the sport while at college and achieved a marathon time of 2:55 in 1978. His love for running at first morphed into a growth stunting addiction. Over time, however, his adoption of interval sprint training as a habit of excellence in conjunction with other forms of mindfulness training increased the self-regulating capacities of a nervous system once destabilized by emotional traumas large and small. Such regulatory flexibility primed Milch to creatively adapt to bigger and bigger challenges once initiated he pursued with passionate vigor.

Milch recently reconnected with his interest in songwriting and performance and released his first CD of original pop music, *Late Bloomer Boomer*, in 2016.

Milch lives with his wife, Laura, in Fair Lawn, New Jersey, and has two grown daughters from a former marriage.